Last Scene Underground

LAST SCENE UNDERGROUND

An Ethnographic Novel of Iran

ROXANNE VARZI

Stanford University Press   Stanford, California

Stanford University Press
Stanford, California

Printed in the United States of America on acid-free, archival-quality paper

Library of Congress Cataloging-in-Publication Data

Varzi, Roxanne, 1971- author.
 Last scene underground : an ethnographic novel of Iran / Roxanne Varzi.
   pages cm
 Includes bibliographical references.
 ISBN 978-0-8047-9622-4 (cloth : alk. paper)--
 ISBN 978-0-8047-9688-0 (pbk. : alk. paper)--
 ISBN 978-0-8047-9689-7 (eBook)
 1. Theater--Political aspects--Iran--Fiction. 2. Youth--Iran--Social life and customs--Fiction. 3. Iran--Politics and government--21st century--Fiction. I. Title.
 PS3622.A79L37 2015
 813'.6--dc23
                     2015027261

Designed by Bruce Lundquist

Typeset at Stanford University Press in 10.25 / 15 Palatino

For Rumi and Kasra

3 Shelly!
fruid, Editor, teacher, love you!
Roxanne Irvine
2016

All the World's a Stage

WILLIAM SHAKESPEARE

A Note to the Reader

If stories have ancestors, or ghosts, then this one's would be the legacy of the Shiraz Theater Festival in the late 1960s in the Iranian city of wine, poetry and nightingales. The festival was the brainchild of the Queen of Iran, who gave the opportunity to cutting-edge international theater directors to do anything they desired, with an endless budget. They showed naked bodies and blew up mini mountains and some were commissioned to make what became *the* plays of their careers, a well-known example being Peter Brook and Tom Hughes, whose experimental play *Orghast* became a major international success. The Queen's tastes ran toward the modern and Western, the avant-garde, which in those days meant a theater of protest. While her husband's regime was busy imprisoning outspoken critics, she was inadvertently supporting and training them, giving them invaluable exposure to the best possible mentors in the world of political theater: Tadeusz Kantor, Jerzy Grotowski, Peter Brook, August Wilson and Eugene Ionesco.

Iranian theater has other even-more-powerful homegrown ghosts haunting the villages and plains of Iran, the most important being the traditional eighth-century Shiite passion play *Ta'ziyeh*, an annual reenactment by locals of the martyrdom of Imam Hussein in the Battle of Karbala (Iraq, 680 A.D.). For centuries, *Ta'ziyeh* has provoked strong emotional audience response. By the time the Shiraz Theater Festival was in full swing, the religious opposition to the Shah was already using *Ta'ziyeh* to stir up support. The Shah responded by all but banning the *Ta'ziyeh*. Which is why it was both strange and useful for him to allow a contained and watered-down, apolitical version of the play at the Festival as both a consolation to the Iranian people who did not approve of all the Western theater and as a bonbon for foreigner directors who were anxious to see an example of the famous *Ta'ziyeh*.

The Islamic Revolution is often viewed as a backward, fundamentalist event that was a backlash to the Shah of Iran's rapid modernization. The Revolution was a political rather than a social backlash that was born of an incredibly modern, intellectual and Western moment in Iranian history. The roots of the Revolution may go back to the desire Iranians had in the 1950s to have a democratic government when they elected a French-educated, free-thinking Prime Minister, Mohammad Mossadegh, who worked tirelessly to nationalize Iranian oil. He was ousted by a CIA coup d'état in 1953 that brought back the Pahlavi monarchy and the Shah of Iran.

The Shah's reign was marked by rapid modernization in terms of infrastructure but not politics, during which he had banned all opposing political parties, censored the press and intellectuals (managing to do so with the aid of a strong secret police), allowed increased inflation to create a large gap between rich and poor and kept an especially keen eye on the clerics who opposed his economic reforms, including the radical young seminarian Ayatollah Khomeini. The Shah saw to Khomeini's worldly education by exiling him first to Iraq and then prophetically to France, where he was exposed to the perfect blend of postcolonial theory, postwar French philosophy and esoteric Islam.

The Iranian Revolution began as a people's movement against the Shah that eventually turned into an Islamic Revolution led by Ayatollah Khomeini. Khomeini could not have pulled off the revolution without the secular liberal intellectuals who paved the ground before him. The Revolution included everyone, from American feminist Kate Millet to a radical antimonarchy movement that encompassed Communists, Islamic Marxists, Islamic guerillas and Islamic feminists. It was a backlash against informal colonialism and imperialism and what Michel Foucault, a French philosopher who was also present at the marches, megaphone in hand, believed initially to be an attempt to insert "spirit into a world without spirit."

In 1980, shortly after the Islamic Revolution, Saddam Hussein attacked Iran, which resulted in a bloody ten-year war. The Iran-Iraq War (1980 to 1989) mobilized a splintered Iranian population against a common enemy, allowing for the new Islamic government to create and consolidate its state. The war became known as the Sacred Defense and the soldiers who died fighting it were elevated to the status of Islamic martyrs. From the outset of the war, a propaganda arm of the new government used *Ta'ziyeh* to play on the Sunni/Shiite split between Iraq and Iran and emphasize the importance of Hussein's martyrdom in order to drum up war support and excite future martyrs. Iran became a cartography of death, mapped by the images of martyrs on the sides of apartment buildings, in highway billboards, on television, local stages and film and as statues in fountains and traffic squares. In the end, over a million people died on both sides, but no borders had shifted, nothing but human flesh was won or lost.

Meanwhile, the new Islamic government was moving full-force ahead in changing the rules for public conduct and enforcing what they believed to be more pious behavior. Women were required to cover their heads with a *russari, hejab* or *magneh* and to wear a traditional full-length chador or a *rupush,* a long coat akin to a raincoat. Men could not wear short sleeves, t-shirts, shorts, baseball caps (at first) or anything too "Western" looking. Cultural rules went into effect, banning activities like chess, coed socializing among unmarried youth, any kind of nontraditional music, and riding bicycles and singing for women. Vigilantes, the *Basij,* and the Islamic police, *Komiteh,* kept an eye on citizens and punished inappropriate dress and behavior.

Despite every effort on the part of youth from secular families to ignore the physical space of state propaganda, some Revolutionary ideals and rules seeped into their psyches regardless. After all, there is no better way to encourage an Islamic citizenry than by making a person physically inseparable from her Islamic city (like wearing Islamic covering). But even so, the state was not wholly effective in turning the population into perfect Islamic citizens; on the contrary, many ignored, turned away from the city and completely detached in public in order to resist the undesirable space. Some simply created alternative spaces inside their own homes and those of others who offered private painting classes, music classes, unsanctioned parties with coed gatherings and alcohol (the prohibition of which only created a strong black market). By the time the youth born at the beginning of the 1979 Revolution came of age, they were well-versed in how a proper Islamic citizen should behave, and were very good at pretending to conform—all the while becoming increasingly weary of leading a double life.

In 1995, the election of the reformist President Mohammad Khatami offered the first indication that the children of the Revolution, now old enough to vote, did not necessarily agree with the revolutionary government. Khatami relaxed the Islamic codes by permitting musical concerts, chess and non-Islamic-themed theater, providing education subsidies and allowing reformist newspapers that critiqued hardliners. He gave youth a chance to come out of hiding and exhibit their art: music, theater, painting and photography, all of which flourished under his regime. But he remained careful and prudent: the dress code, for example, became more relaxed but remained. And women still could not and cannot sing in public.

Unfortunately, not everyone in the government supported him, and by 1999 he was dealing with a strengthening opposition that clamped down on many of his reforms. When the government cut Khatami's education subsidies and closed the reformist newspapers, students protested for the first time since the Revolution. What began as a peaceful demonstration ended in riot, with plain-clothed vigilantes storming the dormitories, kicking in walls, smashing television sets and setting fires. A number of students were killed and imprisoned. It was never clear who ordered the riot police in or why Khatami didn't speak out against the violence. What was clear was that violence changes everything.

After the dormitory protests, Khatami again made more reforms in the press and in education, and even gestures of friendship to the outside world. Unfortunately these were coupled with a failing economy, a scarcity of jobs, disillusionment in the general public marked by a rise in drug use among wealthy teens with nothing else to do and among the poor, who gave their last coins for the sludge at the bottom of wealthy men's opium pipes. Twelve-step recovery programs mushroomed—underground, but overlooked. There was a rise in male and female prostitution, open discussions in the press occurred about HIV and homosexuality and sex change operations were hot topics in the underground media.

In the intellectual sphere, culture was also changing. Philosophical and radical texts from abroad like Foucault's and Heidegger's were being translated into Persian and readily available in bookstores. New Age themes were popular, and the top-selling author of *The Alchemist*, Paulo Coelho, began making annual visits to his readers in Iran. Films from Iran acquired world acclaim and won Oscars. But theater was only just coming into its own as a radical and different art form.

Film and theater had been vital to the creation of a martyrdom culture since the start of the Iran-Iraq War in 1980, making it important for the government to continue to support film schools and drama departments. In Tehran, The Farabi Film Center and the City Theater operated throughout the Revolution, and shortly after the end of the war various congresses on drama, from War Theater to *Ta'ziyeh* and children's theater, puppet-theater and the famous Fajr Theater Festival were formed to especially highlight the works of those film and theater producers who had been active in the war and who continued to make government propaganda. Immediately after the Revolution, a number of cutting-edge playwrights and directors who had made anti-Shah theater (but were not necessarily pro-Islamic Republic) continued to work in the theater and to teach. They made use of traditional methods and narrative conventions such as *pardeh khani*, which involved a storyteller who in the old days rode into town on a donkey with a large sheepskin sheet embellished with the most fantastical scenes from Ferdowsi's *Shahnameh* ("Book of Kings"), which he'd prop up behind him while he recited his mythic tales about the Arab invasion of Persia. After the Revolution, the *Shahnameh* was considered too monarchial, too anti-Islam, until it was reinterpreted in 1989 in Hamid-Reza A'zam's play *The Last Technique,* in which the storyteller read tales rewritten to replace the original characters with heroic young martyrs of the Iran-Iraq War. Aside from war-themed or moral stories, through most of the nineties, public performance consisted of imported Chinese opera with only male actors invited on the stage, classical Persian music concerts with again only male musicians and religious plays like *Ta'ziyeh,* in which all the roles, including female roles, are played by men.

As a result of all the government support for the performance arts, there was an entire generation of filmmakers and actors coming of age by the time of Khatami's election who had skill and talent but not the freedom to perform anything that wasn't sanctioned by the state. With film, it was easier: producers could trick the censors by submitting a script for production, getting the money and a trusted crew and permission and then making a different film in the editing room that could be exported and featured in international film festivals.

Theater was more difficult: it was hard enough to get approval to stage a play in Iran. All plays had to be approved by the government and permission had to be granted to begin rehearsals. And then government censors often crashed the rehearsals. Once a radical performance was premiered it might get shut down immediately, meaning that all the rehearsals and work might only be for one performance. The theater's only exportable product was live performances, but getting government permission for individuals to perform abroad was not easy. International festivals had to agree that there would be no touching and that Iranian women would veil. The Iranian government would collect the performers' passports and government handlers accompanied the groups. Yet, some performers still defected.

In the late 1990s many youth theater companies worked intensely together "underground" as unofficial companies, only coming above ground after Khatami's election. By 1999 they had fully emerged above ground and were for the first time creating an alternative artistic space in the public sphere. I saw this firsthand at Hamed Taheri's production of *The Blacks*, which opened in Tehran in the spring of 2000. *The Blacks* was inspired loosely by Jean Genet's *The Blacks: A Clown Show*, and introduced to Iranian theater some of the first serious body-movement, avant-garde use of sound and text since the Shiraz Theater Festival in the 1970s. Taheri's company had first met nine years earlier in an underground acting and movement class. What made Taheri's theater so pathbreaking was his incorporation of Jerzy Grotowski's incredibly taxing movement and acting method, known as Poor Theater, described by Grotowski in his groundbreaking book *Towards a Poor Theatre* (1968). Taheri had painstakingly trans-

xvi   A Note to the Reader

lated this thirty-year-old text twenty words a day with the help
of an old dog-eared English dictionary. Taheri not only imported
Grotowski's acting exercises but also completely adhered to his
radically antiestablishment ideas of a poor theater. Taheri revo-
lutionized the way theater was being done in Tehran, including
improvisational elements (risky but necessary when scripts were
highly censored), choreography that allowed male and female actors to just barely touch and most important, the addition of audience participation, which got out of control during his last *Blacks*
performances, when female audience members touched male actors and even threw off their veils.

That performance inspired me to think about ways that I too, as
an anthropologist, could push through boundaries—disciplinary,
genre, political and personal—and could write about resistance,
creativity and hope. To that end I spent the next decade research-
ing and writing and rewriting this novel about a group of young
Iranian college students who form an underground avant-garde
theater group and, defying censorship and using other forms of
social resistance, attempt to put on a play. Though this book is inspired by the plays that took place in Tehran primarily at the turn
of the last century, it is not a retelling of those performances. Nor
is it a political commentary about a specific movement, which is
why I further fictionalized the action by placing it in 2009, when
a protest similar to the dormitory protests of 1999 occurred and a
political tug-of-war ensued between the people and the government, with masses of Iranians of all ages taking to the streets.
Writing fiction allows me to stay away from political specificities
that might link a particular theater moment or individual to a particular political moment in time, be it 1999 or 2009. But writing
a fictional ethnography allows me to keep to the ethnographic
specificities at the heart of this theater movement.

What makes this book different from a traditional novel is the
inclusion of the director's notes, which are a fictional notebook

kept by a fictional character. The notes are a culmination of my research, which ranged from people I interviewed and plays that I read and watched to my reflections, observations and interpretations. They assume the responsibility of the writer and anthropologist to inform the story. In short, they are partially a version of my own notes from the field, but fictionalized to the degree that nothing was included that an Iranian character like the director would not himself have known or read. In that sense the novel is an intense collaboration with the people I researched to the end that I remain grounded in fact—even when wanting to move fully into fiction. The book is, to the extent that any ethnography can be, based on research. It is a reflection of daily life—which in Tehran is lived creatively, whether one is an artist or not.

While this book is about collaboration—between fact and fiction, art and ethnography, science and human experience, the anthropologist and the people—it is ultimately about the freedom to create and to openly express our creations, opinions and insights. It is about leaving the dark and moving toward the light.

Last Scene Underground

بسم الله الرحمن الرحيم

In the Name of God

The story begins or ends, depending on whether you open this notebook in English (read left to right) or in Persian (read right to left), with a German newspaper clipping:

A young woman, believed to be Iranian, was found prone on a bed of snow in Berlin's Tiergarten Woods near the House of World Cultures. It appears as though she had been running and fell, but whether it was toward or away from someone or something has yet to be determined. She was taken to a hospital and treated for frostbite, but refuses to speak. The Berlin police request that if you have any information about the woman to please come forward.

Toward or away from? I wish I knew.

Imagine that night: the total and enveloping silence of a growing snowstorm and a woman alone, waiting or escaping, about to fall—a distant figurine in an unbreakable snow-globe.

All that's left of her is this fading foreign newspaper clipping and either the beginning or the end of a story.

Islamic Morals

Leili fidgets anxiously with the zip of her red knapsack in the security line outside the green gates of Tehran University. A student ahead of her decked out in a hot pink russari, veil, refuses to remove her nail polish.

"Come on, you're holding up the line," someone complains behind her.

"Arrest her; I'm late," another man only half jokes.

The flustered guard finally steps aside for a moment and the crowd of angry, late students overtakes the offender and rushes in unchecked. Leili moves as quickly as she can without breaking into a totally improper run, across the courtyard, into the Faculty of Science building and all the way to the top floor, where she walks into class late and out of breath.

The professor's back is turned to the chalkboard, where she very carefully pens "The downtrodden will be rewarded in paradise," as Leili slips behind a mountain of students who descend in stadium seats toward the lectern.

The professor turns, wipes her brow with the back of her hand, smudging her thick black chador with chalk dust, and eyes Leili, examining for a moment her black russari and plain jeans—nothing worth reporting.

The classroom is filled to capacity. Islamic Morals is an elective but not a choice.

A young religious woman in a perfectly pressed black chador, round gold reading glasses and lips that smack of waxy ChapStick glares at Leili. Another religious student with a tightly trimmed beard and neatly stacked reference books at the ready also eyes her. She turns her gaze toward the slouched and half-asleep long-haired hipster next to him who wears black jeans and colorful Pumas. If he slouches any farther, he might slip out of his seat or fall over onto the person next to him—a young, handsome man in a loose-fitting oxford, black pants and the kind of religious bushy beard that announces that he's not here to study. Leili makes a mental note to avoid him; she wishes that he were the one slouched and asleep, but he's awake, alert and observing her.

No seat in sight, Leili turns to exit when a chadored student stands and offers Leili her seat.

The professor witnesses the exchange. "Sit," she tells the *chadori*. Then she looks Leili in the eye and says, "There are always extra seats available for the willing." She is already dragging and banging a metal folding chair across the stone floor to the center of the room where she stops and waits for Leili to join her.

Leili perches on the edge of the chair, aware that her too short and too colorful baby blue *rupush* is inching up her thighs and exposing her Levi's. She feels a hundred eyes on her back and her professor's steady gaze overhead as she pulls out her notebook and neatly pens "In the Name of God"—بسم الله الرحمن الرحيم. She looks up, ready to take notes. Satisfied, the professor walks swiftly back to the chalkboard. Leili detects a click of high heels under the swish of her chador.

At the chalkboard she turns dramatically to the class and begins her lecture. "Essence, Islamic essence," she says. "Does carrying prayer beads and muttering prayers aloud for all to see make a man right with God?"

"No," the professor answers her own question. "Does throw-

ing coins into the alms depositories as you enter the highway
protect you for your journey if you do it while playing loud hip-
hop music?"

Once the professor is ensconced in the day's lecture, Leili begins her doodles. From doodling she progresses to her lists. Groceries: eggplant, onions, tomatoes, cucumbers, lemons, lettuce;
paints—she needs new paints for Saturday's class—crimson,
ochre, mustard, ash . . . cigarettes for her father. She thinks of
him sitting alone at home staring into the smoke, and a little dark
cloud passes over her.

Her professor's voice projects to make an important point:

"*Riyah* . . . showing off a religious demeanor, like thumbing
prayer beads while thinking of your girlfriend, or giving alms
just for self-protection or . . ."

Veiling . . . Leili thinks, remembering a woman defiantly riding a motorcycle and wearing a cherry-red helmet through rush
hour traffic. She smiles to herself. She closes her eyes and imagines herself speeding through Tehran on a motorbike past the
only uncovered female creatures in the city—the tall, slender
cypress trees that rise out of the *joobs*, wide open ditches along
the street. A dark oval that stains the white bark of every cypress
forms an eye that watches Leili as she floats by in her daydream.

"Riyah," the professor repeats.

Leili opens her eyes and returns to writing her list. Nuts—
she needs trail mix for her hike this weekend: raisins (the long
green ones), dried mulberries, pistachios and cashews or walnuts
(fresh ones, already shelled). It's walnut season now. When the
page is nearly filled and the hour almost over, Leili prickles at a
smell of imported deodorant, a collision of lavender and Clorox.
She looks up to find her professor standing over her. It's too late
to slam the notebook shut.

"I asked you a question," her professor says sharply.

Leili clears her throat.

A slight smile crawls across her professor's lips as she tells the class to repeat the question.

Leili's cheeks burn, her pulse rushes, her stomach turns.

"When is it appropriate for a layperson to interpret a spiritual leader's decrees?" the students recite in unison.

Leili knows the answer is "Never." She glances down at her notebook and shifts in her seat. Her chest thumps. She fingers her gold chain, feeling for the delicate cross beneath her shirt. The cross beats back and forth against her chest like an out-of-whack pendulum or fleeting prayer. She imagines herself wearing a cherry-red helmet. She sees a whirl of tall white cypresses speed by her with their steady watching eyes and she whispers, "Always."

There's a collective gasp from the room.

Her professor glares at her. "You misheard. I did not ask when it is *not* appropriate, but when it *is* appropriate to interpret a text," the woman says, waiting for Leili to play along.

Leili raises her eyes to meet her professor's glare and feeling slightly queasy says, "A person should be free to make her own interpretations."

"Even of God's Word?" the professor snaps.

Leili nods slightly and immediately feels all of her blood rush to her head.

Her professor solemnly walks back to the blackboard and slowly and deliberately erases the board. The hollow of held breaths, the rhythm of the professor's eraser, back and forth, back and forth, wool on slate in rhythm with her short, tight staccato breaths and Leili's fingernail scraping intently at a speck of gum on her metal desk echo loudly in the otherwise still classroom.

When only the word *paradise* remains, the professor turns and orders them out: "Dismissed."

Leili is frozen to her seat as waves of students rush past all around her. Only one student pauses long enough to catch her eye—the bearded student studies her for a moment and then smiles before walking away.

Leili stands limply.

She mutters "with your permission" as she walks past her professor's turned back.

Without turning to face Leili, the professor says, "Watch yourself—others will not be so tolerant to one who disrespects the principles for which so many of our young martyrs died."

Leili clears her throat to speak.

"Go." Her professor has spoken.

Murals

Night comes and with it crowds as thick as Tehran's pollution. Neon warning signs tell the elderly, people with pacemakers and pregnant women to stay home. A crowd of students moves like a colony of black ants in and out of bookstores, the cinema (where a silly comedy is playing), the music store (where sheet music is stacked below hanging sitars), the pizzerias, cafés and a professional art store. Leili pauses to admire the alluring jars of brilliantly ground pigments that glimmer in the fading light— titanium, cerulean, cobalt and manganese—colors as vibrant as their names. She feels a tap on her shoulder and jumps.

"Sorry," an older woman apologizes, "I thought you were someone else."

"It's OK, I was . . . just . . . ," Leili starts to say, but the woman has already been swept into the mad rush hour crowd.

Three days it has taken Leili to summon the courage since her outburst in class to come close to the university district and now she's determined to get home as quickly as she can.

Her parents thinks she's in class until six, so she takes the long way home, a more secluded route, winding up hilly Mohammed Beg Street where the climb is steep and the recently paved tar is still cushiony hot. Every few steps she looks behind her, but every second man has a beard—none of them as young or as handsome as the one in class.

Her russari and rupush are already unknotted and unbuttoned

as she walks through the apartment door. "I'm home," she calls, turning on lights as she moves down the silent and dark hall.

"Out here," her mother, Saqi, calls back.

Leili walks through the large receiving room, past the kitchen to the balcony, where her mother stands to greet her.

Leili hugs her cushiony mother tightly.

"What's wrong?" Saqi asks.

"Nothing," Leili whispers. She peers over the balcony rail to avoid her mother's eyes. Tehran sprawls beneath them: a cosmos of skyscrapers, snow-capped peaks and a smog-induced ultraviolet sunset that obscures the city's underbelly of propaganda.

"Ever notice we can't see the murals from up here?" Leili says without turning.

"The murals?" Saqi sucks in her dimples and gives her daughter a concerned look.

"The martyrs." They're too far up for that kind of detail. Tehranis who can afford to can escape almost anything.

"Since when were you concerned about the martyrs?" Saqi stares hard at Leili.

"I'm not. Just class."

"Are they still teaching you about martyrs in college? The endless war, over and over. It's all they know how to teach. Depressing the young who don't even remember." Saqi frowns. "Needless murder and now endless reminders."

"I'm going in," Leili says, trying not to imagine her professor's voice joined by an assembly of a dozen disrespected dead boys asking her, why? Why she has the right to aimlessly walk the streets, to escape, while they're stuck on the wall for the duration of the cheap paint's life. Why do you get to live? she imagines them asking her. What makes your life so valuable? Storm clouds gather slowly in the higher peaks of the Alborz and depression settles back in like a cat in a comfortable and familiar old chair.

"Leili, it's late." Her father ambles into the sitting room with a tray of tea.

She clears her throat. "I stopped at Sefat's," she lies.

"I hope you didn't tell her anything." He straightens his back and readjusts the tray.

"There's nothing to tell," she says. "No need to look at me like that; I didn't stay for coffee." She takes his tray and kisses his forehead.

"That nosey neighbor only reads coffee cup fortunes to extract gossip. She's a charlatan." He settles into his winged leather armchair and reaches for the evening paper. A cloud of cigarette smoke forms around him. "There's a chill in the air; it must be fall," he says, exhaling smoke. He wears gray flannel slacks that he has owned since the 1970s (the only ones without cigarette burns), a yellowing V-necked undershirt and black nylon dress socks.

Sitting across from him in the evenings, holding her tea in both hands, feet curled up beneath her and waiting pointlessly for her father's stories of Marxist and mystic friends was a pastime of hers, a daily ritual based on a distant memory of her father telling her bedtime stories as a child. A memory she's not so sure ever happened.

"Some poetry?" she bargains.

"Hmmm . . ." He looks up at her.

Where'd they go, the stories? she wants to ask but never does. Are they stuck deep in his throat waiting to choke him? Or have they, like her, sat here vigilantly for a decade waiting for him to clear his throat?

"Grab a section." He nods to the paper. She pulls at a loose thread from her faded pink sweater. The wool is stained and feels coarse beneath her hand.

"You OK?" her father asks her.

She looks up at him.

"Did I startle you?" he presses her.

"You shaved . . . cologne?" She tries to smile.

He waves the newspaper at her. It's today's paper.

"You went out?" she observes.

"They've consolidated the police, the Basij and the Komiteh. Imagine! Now citizens will no longer know who is protecting them and who is out to get them. Can't trust anyone," he tells her. He roughly folds the paper and places it on the table next to him. He sits back in his chair, crosses his legs and looks at his daughter.

The phone rings but neither moves to answer it.

"No one calls for me," her father comments.

"I'm not in the mood to talk to anyone," Leili answers.

"Is it school?"

"School?"

"Your sudden antisocial mood." He smiles wryly. "You look worried."

She pauses for a moment before saying, "Things are changing and . . ." She nods nervously toward the folded paper for emphasis.

"What do you mean?" He leans forward to study her. "What's this interest in politics?"

She bites her lip. "The police," she says carefully. "Students don't like it—there's talk at school, that's all."

"Of course not," he agrees, and the moment to tell him about her transgression comes and goes as rapidly and innocuously as a missed heartbeat—a murmur one notices only after it has killed.

New Heights

"Tajrish!" Leili calls to the passing cabs. She makes a circular motion with her hand pointing north. A bright orange Peykan Taxi finally pulls over. She jumps in and slams the cheap metal door shut.

"Easy, lady." The driver turns in his seat to reprimand her. He pats the closed back door like a wounded animal and turns to put the car in gear.

Tajrish Square is a whirlwind of activity. In all four corners people disembark from taxis: naturalists with binoculars dangling from their necks, children running free within a safe radius of their parents, older exercise buffs leaning on wooden walking sticks, mothers, students and servants scurrying toward their destinations. A middle-aged male hiking club uniformed in matching khaki calf-length balloon pants, argyle socks and hefty hiking boots, as if they're in the Alps, steadily pass a group of chadored women who are headed to the opposite side of the square toward the Mosque. Leili watches the women deftly slip along in plastic slippers, their chadors securely held in clamped jaws to free their hands for bags and babies.

Leili squeezes into the small rusting minibus that takes weekenders up the mountain and dumps them at the feet of the once-majestic and forbidding giant bronze statue of a hiker that was erected in the Shah era above and beyond a barren plateau. Now it's just another, though larger, figure lost in the chaos of a typical weekend traffic jam where her friends wait patiently for her to join them.

"Where have you been? You've missed three days of class." They start before Leili's even said hello.

"Take it easy. Our professor is hardly the type to admit to her superiors that a pupil contradicted her," one of them defends Leili.

"True," Shadi, her oldest friend, admits.

"It's not her I'm worried about. There was a Basij," Leili tells them.

"What?"

"In class," Leili whispers.

"No! I was decked out and no one stopped me," Shadi comments.

"I noticed," Leili says. "He had a big beard . . ."

"So do half the guys in that class."

"He was watching. He got a good look at my face."

Shadi straightens the visor over her russari, tilting it so a tease of bleached hair falls out. The visor says "Hilton Head Island," though she's never left the city, let alone the country.

"Lighten up, Leili. You're being paranoid." Shadi points them toward the dusty path up the mountain.

They hike up the mountain to Hajji's: a nook of wood platforms covered with Persian rugs, nestled off the edge of the trail with an amazing view of the gray craggy cliffs.

They sit cross-legged and expectantly, hiking boots off and lined up alongside one of the low platforms while Hajji's helper lifts a heavy round metal tray of clanking teacups, fresh hot bread, whipped butter, apricot jam, dates and a plate of fried eggs swimming in melted butter into the middle of their circle.

"Can you believe a cappuccino in Tehran costs the same as in New York City?" Shadi says.

"Since when have you been to New York?" a friend jokes.

"Seriously; Arian told me," Shadi says with authority. "The rial is diving . . ."

"Arian?" Leili asks.

Shadi blushes. "I'll fill you in later."

The girls laugh.

"I can't afford a cappuccino, let alone the TOEFL exam," a friend comments.

"Did you sign up?" Shadi turns to Leili, whose gaze is directed at the mountains and away from the group.

"Leili?" Shadi insists.

"Yes?" Leili stammers, looking back at Shadi.

"Nothing." Shadi looks away.

When breakfast is over Leili waits in a bathroom stall and listens until Shadi has given up looking for her.

A little old man in baggy pants and a torn sweater says, "I told them that you had already headed back down." Hajji winks at her. "Your friends paid," he tells her when she tries to give him money.

"Thank you," Leili says. She looks around the little garden.

Hajji sets down his heavy tray of dirty dishes and straightens his back. "You can beat them down the mountain if you take the chairlift."

Leili's eyes widen. "Too high."

"Why are you climbing mountains if you're afraid of heights?" Hajji grins, revealing a mouth full of gold caps.

"I want some peace and quiet."

"There's a nice waterfall on the path to the right; you'll pass over a narrow bridge. I won't lie to you; it's a steep fall. But if you want time to yourself that's the way."

Leili winds her way up the mountain past the little penny arcades, pausing to sample blackberries and mulberries sold from large baskets along the road by old men bent with age. At a small tea shack she chooses an especially large translucent sheet of tart dried apricot that hangs for sale from a rope. She licks it like a child as she continues up the mountain past all the shops and the last lift station until she's completely alone and deep into a series of strenuous switchbacks.

"Fortunes!" She hears a boy's voice call out. She stops and looks back at a boy of ten or twelve holding a caged canary and a cardboard tray of tiny dirty sealed envelopes.

He sets the cage down, catches his breath and says, "Ten rials for a Hafez fortune."

Leili hands the boy a coin and he pulls the canary out of her cage and gently balances her on his dirty slender finger. The bird bends over the tray and gingerly pecks at a thin envelope. Leili takes the dusty envelope from the bird and pulls out her already faded fortune.

"I can barely read it."

The boy shrugs. "They got rained on."

"Thanks," she says and reads the faint line from Hafez, who promises Leili "The green sea of heaven, the hull of the new moon." Leili pockets the fortune.

One foot in front of the other, she follows the zigzag path higher and higher until the mountainside becomes brown and barren and the cold air pinches at her cheeks like a determined aunt. It doesn't take her long to reach the bridge. She chews a last bite of her fruit disk and wipes her hands on her rupush.

The narrow plank of splintering wood that she steps onto could be a bridge or a shoot straight into the waterfall, depending on her balance. She glances down into the deep abyss of the shiny, wet brown gorge and her pulse quickens. She takes a quick step back, turns and comes face-to-face with the handsome beard from class. Her eyes immediately lower obediently, piously, and as they do, she notices that he is clutching a book of Furugh Farokhzad's poetry—confiscated from some unlucky soul, no doubt.

She looks back up at him. His nose and cheeks are red from running. He's wearing blue jeans and a peacoat. He smiles at her the same way he did in class.

"Don't give up," he says.

"I . . ." Leili hesitates.

"You won't fall if you keep your eyes up and straight ahead of you. Promise," he reassures her.

"I've lost my friends," Leili says, looking past him.

He steps close to her, and she smells not the expected sour scent of mosque rosewater but bergamot and pine.

"Really? No one's come by here. Sure you didn't ditch them?" His eyes twinkle.

She furrows her brow. He smiles, but doesn't budge. "It's difficult to lose someone on a one-way path unless you really try. There's always someone breathing down your neck," he says lightly.

"Yup." Leili steps back. Her heart pounds.

"Vertigo."

"What?"

"Fear, desire. You're afraid to fall but something has you wondering what it would be like if you just . . ." He peers over the edge.

"Desire?" Leili blushes.

"To jump. I'm Hooman," he says and extends his hand to her. "You *were* going to cross the bridge, no?" His hand remains extended. "You won't fall," he gently urges her.

"Arrest me, go ahead, but I'm not crossing the bridge with you," Leili says defiantly.

"Arrest you? Are you on the run?" Hooman looks around mockingly and laughs.

Leili takes a tentative step back and loses her balance. Hooman drops the book and grabs her arm; his book slips off the bridge and noiselessly falls into the gully.

"Oh no," Leili mutters.

"It was you or the book." Hooman tightens his grip on Leili's arm for emphasis.

"Tough choice. That book's banned." Leili half-smiles.

"Aren't you?"

"Not yet. The professor forgave me."

"But I haven't seen you in class."

"I was avoiding you."

He lets go of her. "Me?"

"I thought . . ." Leili bites her lip and smiles stupidly at him. "I thought you were a Basij," she says.

"Seriously?" Hooman laughs. "Why? Because I smiled at you? Hell, if I were going to arrest you, I'd have done it by now."

"I wish you had. I've been walking around for the past few days afraid of my own shadow."

"That's no way to live," Hooman says gravely.

Leili blinks and says, "I don't know what I was thinking, speaking back to a teacher."

"You don't look the type. I was surprised for sure." Hooman adds, "Brave move, especially in an Islamic morals class."

"Not brave, stupid. I was scared to death, pretending to be brave."

"You can be brave and scared. Pretending's a good start."

"Hmm," Leili answers. She's stopped caring about consequences and wonders if that kind of apathy will lead to worse kinds. She studies his earnest gaze. "You're too smart to be a Basij. You sound like you've actually read a book."

"Want me to grunt some religious platitudes? I'm fluent." Hooman laughs. "You regret it?" He pulls out a cigarette.

"Here?" Leili protests, eyeing the drop. "If you're not going to arrest me, let's get off this bridge." She extends her hand to him. He raises his eyebrows and playfully asks, "Really?"

"This is the scary part," she explains.

Hooman drops her hand gently without ceremony on the other side of the bridge and lights his cigarette. They continue to walk slowly up the trail.

"Sorry about your book," Leili says.

"It's OK, I've memorized it."

"You like Furugh's poetry?"

"I love it. There's a line I thought of when I first saw you in class."

Leili blushes.

"Concealed in me is a sea, how could I hide it? How could I describe it?" Hooman recites.

"If I'm concealing anything it's a puddle, not a sea."

Hooman takes an orange from his pocket and peels it. A sweet smell of citrus hangs tantalizingly in the heavy cold air. He hands half to Leili, "For a successful crossing."

Leili delicately sections off a piece, puts it in her mouth and makes a sour face.

"Look over there." Hooman points down at Tehran. The city looks like a worn and dusty topographical map with sparse dots of red, orange and brown, dwarfed by the large unshapely patches of gray concrete.

"It looks so far away," she says.

"Unreal," says Hooman.

They reach an altitude where words freeze and only silence is buoyant.

"We need to hurry if we're going to make it down by sunset." Hooman motions for her to turn.

Leili inhales the fading scent of pine needle, and memorizes the fresh smell of green. "OK," she agrees reluctantly and follows him down the mountain.

It feels like no time has passed before they're at the super-sized bronze hiker and Hooman says, "This is good-bye."

"Thank you," Leili says.

"Come to Café Naderi Monday afternoon. We'll read banned books and practice pretending," Hooman promises.

No Wings to Fly to God

Leili glances down into the joob as she walks along the sidewalk; she's too far north to see anything but burnt-orange and red leaves spinning their way to the treeless south, where fall arrives through the gutters. Today the force and pressure of the rainwater rushing through the joobs means snow in the Alborz has covered the bridge that Leili and Hooman crossed on Friday.

By the time she reaches Jomhuri Street in the south, the metal store shutters along the block of electronic shops that front banned media sellers have already come down like heavy eyelids for the afternoon siesta. A siesta that doesn't apply to the black market moneychangers who slither past her in their satin vests with bulging pockets and lewdly whisper *dollar* as if they're offering sex.

The "Café" sign looks like it hasn't stopped rusting since the 1940s, when Café Naderi was the place to plot, pen and paint (mostly for Marxist writers).

The air in the café is smoky and warm and the yellow glow of a dimly lit chandelier spills down the pink nicotine-stained walls of the large square room. The high ceilings eagerly echo crowded conversations from a scattering of card tables around the sparsely decorated room.

Hooman sits alone at a large round table with head bent over a spiral notebook, furiously scribbling. His untouched cigarette burns away in a glass ashtray near his wrist. Without lifting his eyes off his work, he says hello.

"Are you clairvoyant?" Leili laughs.

He looks up, shrugs and pulls a chair out for her. She hangs her wool shawl on the chair's slender wood shoulders and looks around.

The same old hunk of reliable metal that brewed espresso for Tehran's now-dead literati gurgles and spits at the clean glasses lined up neatly along the salmon-colored Formica bar.

Hooman watches her carefully. "Haven't you been here before?" he asks.

Leili is flushed and breathless from the walk. She looks out the French doors. "They're lovely."

"They lead to a garden where they had massive parties with twenty-piece bands."

"Parties?"

"Before the Revolution." Hooman looks outside. "It's going to storm," he says.

"I hope so. I love watching angry storms from big safe windows. To be in the midst of thrashing branches and torrential rain—yet protected. As if in an aquarium."

"A fish?" Hooman laughs.

"When I told my father where I was headed this afternoon he insisted that the café was destroyed after the Revolution and that all I'd find is the old sign. He thinks life ended after the Revolution."

"One of those," Hooman remarks.

"When I was in elementary school he'd take me to a café on our street for a café glacé when I got a good grade."

"So he does go out?"

"Well . . ." Leili looks at her lap.

"I get it, the grades went south?"

Leili laughs.

"This is where your type hangs out," Hooman says.

"My type?"

"Artists."

Leili blushes. "I'm not really an artist, I'm just . . . I like paint-ing." Looking around at the Bohemian-chic women with intense kohl-lined eyes who have gotten away with wearing silk bandan-nas as veils and flowing velvet capes, she wonders if the motor-cyclist with the cherry-red helmet hangs out here.

"This place is special," Hooman says. "Furugh Farokhzad hung out here." Hooman looks up at her and recites Furugh from memory:

My whole being is a dark chant which will carry you . . .
in this chant I grafted you to the tree, to the water, to the fire.

"Maybe Furugh wrote the poem in the chair you're sitting in," Hooman jokes.

Leili's cheeks burn. "Do they make café glacé here?" she asks. She looks around for a waiter to avoid Hooman's intense gaze.

"Yup, they still serve café glacé, even to adulterous women," Hooman teases.

"And men." Leili adds, "A fallen woman never falls alone and besides, Furugh was single, he was the one who was married."

Leili studies a woman at a nearby table. Hooman follows her gaze. "She's a sculptor."

Leili looks back at Hooman and whispers, "The woman sitting with the three younger women?"

"Private drawing class."

"Here?"

Hooman nods.

A tuft of silver hair falls from the sculptress's russari and brushes the corner of her right eye. The silver of her hair against her tanned skin reminds Leili of a photograph her father once made of a piece of driftwood on sand.

"She must have been pretty when she was younger."

"Younger? How old do you think she is?" Hooman asks.

The sculptress's smile lines are pulled into an austere and intimidating frown. "Fifty?" Leili ventures.

"Thirty-five."

"Really?" Leili takes a second look at the woman.

"Not easy for women artists . . ."

"Are you trying to discourage me?"

"On the contrary."

"You know that every Friday there are at least ten gallery openings?" Leili insists.

"Not of nudes," Hooman says definitively. "That's the beauty of the government. They allow some things to thrive so as not to draw attention to everything else that they're suffocating." Hooman pauses and takes on a gentler tone. "She's not suffocating; she's just not . . . public. She has an amazing studio in her home. I'll take you some time."

"You've been?" Leili's eyes widen.

"Not to pose."

"I didn't . . ." Leili blushes and swiftly gestures to his notebook, changing the subject. "What are you writing?"

"Notes, translations, thoughts—kind of a journal of the project."

"Project?"

"As soon as the others come I'll explain it to you."

"Others?"

"A few friends."

"Oh . . ."

The waiter finally arrives. "What will you have?" he barks impatiently.

"Café glacé, please."

"In this weather? A hot espresso or a cappuccino, maybe?" The waiter taps his pencil on his pad; his maroon barbershoplike smock is perfectly pressed despite the hours he's been at work. Thirty-odd customers wait at ten other tables.

"Well . . ." Leili hesitates. Hooman frowns in disapproval.

"The glacé, please," Leili says, and nods for emphasis.

"Another double espresso, please."

A clean-cut, classically handsome college student with tight curly black hair and a warm smile approaches their table and catches the waiter as he's leaving.

"Latte," he orders. He looks decidedly out of place in his polo shirt and dress shoes but doesn't seem to notice or care as he sets down his workout duffel and pats Hooman on the back.

"Hey, Nima," Hooman greets him. Nima smiles and peers down at Hooman's notebook. Hooman quickly shuts the notebook and pulls out an empty chair.

"Nima, Leili—Leili, Nima. Leili and I met in Islamic Morals class," Hooman says. "Why don't you two get to know one another? I have another paragraph to translate."

"If he spent half the time on engineering that he spends translating passages out of obscure European texts . . . ," Nima starts.

"Engineering?" Leili interrupts.

"Yeah, don't we look like engineers?" Nima asks.

"I assumed philosophy or literature."

Nima laughs and says, "You have him pegged. No, Hooman? You have no intention of being an engineer—no need to dress the part or show up for class." Hooman ignores him.

"He scored too high on the concourse to be dumped in the arts faculty," Nima says, taking a napkin and wiping the table.

"Here we are thirty years into a Revolution that supposedly purged all Western elements from our culture and we're still stuck taking a damn French-style college entrance exam," Hooman mutters.

"It suits him, this endless road to graduation. Gets him out of military service."

Hooman looks back down at his notes.

"How?" Leili asks. "Can't you just buy it off?" she asks Hooman.

"Not everyone has the money," Hooman retorts.

"He purposely fails Islamic Morals every year," Nima explains.

"I'll stay until I'm old enough to be exempt," Hooman adds.

"You're kidding." Leili looks at Hooman. "Isn't the exemption age forty?"

"What else am I going to do until forty? There's no employment and I can't leave without a passport."

"And you?" Nima asks Leili.

"Electrical, Tehran," she says, and then, "though I'd prefer to be dumped in the arts faculty."

"You're still in school?"

"Aren't you?"

"No," Nima says. "I graduated, did my military service." He pats Hooman on the back for emphasis. "I work at my uncle's company . . ." Nima's distracted by a tall woman, obscured by the hood of a long black crepe cape, who glides effortlessly toward their table. The woman's hood slips to reveal a swath of dark indigo silk wrapped tightly around her head. A delicate layer of moisture films her exposed forehead. Her nose is long and prominent and her lashes are so thick that her eyes almost look like slats, like a cat's, half-opened.

"She practices the intimidating glare," Nima whispers to Leili.

"Arezoo?" Hooman asks without looking up.

"Yup," Nima says. "She walks around with books on top of her head," Nima teases, and he and Hooman chuckle.

Leili tries not to stare. She isn't the only one. Arezoo is a walking magnet that grabs every set of eyes she passes. She isn't classically attractive, but she has presence.

When she reaches their table, Arezoo gently lands in an empty seat without disturbing her perfect posture. She smiles at Nima and Hooman and glares at Leili.

"Actress?" Arezoo looks Leili up and down—her eyes settle

on the little string that Leili picks at on her sleeve. Leili slips her hands under the table.

"I'm an engineering student," Leili says.

Arezoo looks away dismissively and says to Hooman, "I have the perfect male actor for us."

"Really?" Nima looks at Hooman.

"Yes."

"Can he be trusted?" Nima asks.

"Of course," Arezoo says.

"Listen up. I'm translating some radical Polish theater exercises," Hooman says and looks up at them and shuts his book. "Cool stuff! The performance will be extremely physical," Hooman begins.

"Sure, of course it will, because you won't be participating," Nima jabs.

Hooman ignores him and continues: "It involves modern dance, yoga and a few different theater philosophies. The audience will participate. They will sit on stage with us."

Nima laughs. "In what corner of the earth will an audience do that? And will they give us a visa?"

"Here—we're doing it right here in Tehran. Enough frozen body syndrome."

"You do realize that no one has changed the laws? We still can't swing our hips or touch each other—or did I miss something?"

"It's time to use our bodies artistically. We'll figure out a way. Someone has to," Hooman says.

"Theater?" Leili asks.

"Leili *joon*, dear, you're at a theater rehearsal," Hooman pronounces.

Leili looks at Nima and knits her brows. "News to me as well," Nima says curtly.

Arezoo straightens her back against the chair and for the first time turns to face Leili. She looks her directly in the eyes and says,

"Hooman makes his actors earn their place in the production. We work like dogs. Even at the Thespian Academy we didn't work so hard."

"I'm not an actor," says Leili. "Are you?" she asks Hooman.

Arezoo lightly taps out a drum roll on the table and with a Friday Night Newscaster singsong, recounts how she first met Hooman:

"It was just after Nowruz, at the vernal equinox, when the Japanese plum trees in Naderi's garden were in full bloom that midway through a particularly riveting passage of *Henry V*, a strong scent of jasmine disturbed our young hero's equilibrium of coffee and cigarettes."

"Arezoo, really," Hooman protests.

She continues: "The simple provincial boy looked up at a young woman dressed in a sleek, fitted, chic rupush and asked, 'Did you say something?' She retorted, 'Are you preparing to audition?' He gave her a quizzical look. He set down his book to give her his full attention. He seldom paid attention to other people, though women always noticed him. He had looks that made young girls giggle." She glances at Leili.

Nima laughs.

"Arezoo, stop," Hooman says, laughing.

She continues: "Women sense his underlying intensity and rarely brave a word with him."

"Okay, enough, Arezoo. Really, Islamic Republic Broadcasting should ban those monotone newscasters from television forever," Nima says. He shifts uncomfortably in his seat.

"Oh, but they're so Islamic Republic," Hooman says, and winks at Leili.

"The kitsch certainly suits contemporary Tehran," Leili adds dryly.

"Once we figured out that Hooman wasn't in reality an actor, we invited him to join us to read the play anyway—we were short of men."

"Short of men? Arezoo, it was my impression that you were the only woman," Hooman remarks.

"This really happened?" asks Leili.

"You can't blame me for mistaking Hooman for an actor. I mean, look at him . . . the almond-shaped eyes, delicate hands and chiseled cheekbones. Pale skin and dark hair. The hair, all that beautiful hair. That was before he cut his ponytail and grew a beard," Arezoo comments. Leili blushes. Arezoo clearly enjoys the effect she has on men. She sighs. "Anyway, I passed his table on my way back from the lady's room and noticed that under those long black lashes he was reading Shakespeare. So I pointed across the salon to our group huddled around a single battered paperback copy of Shakespeare—in case he should have the wrong impression of my friendly advances."

"Now, why would anyone have the wrong impression of your friendly advances?" Hooman asks. Nima smiles tightly.

"You guys were reading *Taming of the Shrew*. That's hardly the same thing or a coincidence. It's a completely different beast," Hooman says.

"Yeah, a real coincidence considering we needed another male actor and you happened to be reading a Shakespeare play," Arezoo says, her eyes narrow. Leili decides that Arezoo must regard everyone with suspicion.

"I assure you, it was a coincidence. Not everyone who reads a play wants to act, or direct, for that matter," Hooman retorts. He takes a long drag on his cigarette and then taps it on the edge of the ashtray.

"Shakespeare is monarchist—it's banned. It's quite a *coincidence*." Arezoo emphasizes the word *coincidence* and stares back at him.

"Shakespeare is hardly in short supply. Where do you think all those banned books landed after the Revolution?"

"The black market," Leili thinks aloud. "And besides, it's no longer banned. Did you see the performance last year?"

"The one where they don't really say anything?" Hooman remarks.

Arezoo ignores them and mocks: "What did he say . . . 'I'm reading Freud, and he's led me back to the Greeks. Shakespeare makes more sense after you read the Greeks.'" She laughs. "First of all, who talks like that? And besides, Freud is banned. I think Hooman saw one of the calls we posted for actors."

"Calls? Where would you post a call for a theater group practicing a banned play?" Leili asks.

"Graffiti, coded. Spray-painted on a wall, like along the Darband hiking trail, for example," Arezoo says matter-of-factly.

Leili glances at Hooman.

He feigns helplessness. "She wouldn't leave. She was relentless."

"I bought him a coffee," Arezoo says. They all laugh.

"I really had no choice after that," Hooman says. He stares down at his notebook and pretends to be engrossed in his work.

"We placed calls for actors in strategic locations across the city—in Naderi's bathroom, in the Uni bathrooms, on walls—but it took a while. Our flyers were torn down or spray painted over by the Komiteh." Arezoo pauses, catches her breath and continues: "Word of mouth got us enough actors eventually. In the meantime, Hooman convinced us to rehearse *Henry V* in case our only chance was to perform at the Week of Remembrance for the War Festival." Arezoo glances at Nima.

"Are you serious?" Leili asks.

"*Henry V* is about war," Hooman remarks.

"By the time we had cast the play, Hooman had memorized all of it," Nima adds.

"He clutched his copy of Shakespeare tightly and circled the stage with directions, corrections and forgotten lines. During pauses and pockets of silence he spoke to us of Shakespeare. He spoke softly . . . ," Arezoo lowers her voice to a hush for emphasis, "which forced us all to stand *very* close, and to concentrate *very* hard on his *every* word."

"No," Hooman protests, his nose still buried in his notebook.

"It's true," Nima agrees.

"By the time he had the confidence to project his voice, there was an invisible bubble around our little group, with him at the center." Arezoo pauses. "No one dared speak during rehearsal, but outside, in the university drama department, we admitted to each other that the more we practiced, the more we wanted to run. One day, I couldn't hold back—I suggested that maybe we just weren't brave enough, that this was too much to handle. Well, you can imagine our director's stoic expression as he replied, 'You need to use your diaphragm; your voice should be much deeper.'" Arezoo mimics Hooman's low tenor:

> God of battles! Steel my soldiers' hearts;
> Possess them not with fear; take from them now
> The sense of reckoning, if the opposed numbers
> Pluck their hearts from them.

"And battle we did," recalls Arezoo.

"Stop," Hooman insists. He looks up abruptly, but Arezoo ignores him.

"We're just getting started," Arezoo insists.

"Don't," Hooman demands. He slams the notebook shut. Leili jerks slightly in her chair. Arezoo smirks.

"We were shut down at act one," Nima says.

"We practiced all summer only to perform for two government workers," Arezoo says.

"Possibly janitors by the looks of their plastic slippers. They loudly slurped over-brewed tea out of plastic cups during our performance," Nima adds.

"Who were they?" Leili asks.

"The censor board," Arezoo laughs. "They told us Shake-speare is banned."

"Shakespeare is still banned," Leili says matter-of-factly, thinking *what did you expect?*

"Well, it was supposed to be *inspired* by Shakespeare. Hooman told us his translation was *transformed*. It was only later that I realized we were doing a verbatim of King Henry the V's monologue," Nima says. He recites from memory:

> Besides, there is no king, be his cause never so spotless, if it come to the arbitrament of swords, can try it out with all unspotted soldiers. Some, peradventure, have on them the guilt of premeditated and contrived murder; some, of beguiling virgins with the broken seals of perjury; some, making the wars their bulwark, that have before gored the gentle bosom of peace with pillage and robbery. Now, if these men have defeated the law and outrun native punishment, though they can outstrip men, they have no wings to fly from God.

Nima falls silent.

Hooman looks up from his closed notebook and says, "The story parallels that of Imam Hussein on the battlefield of Karbala—it's about just war, a sacred defense, like the Iranians being attacked by Iraq." He pauses. "There was no reason for them to ban it."

"But they did," Nima says.

Leili shifts uncomfortably. "Why the war?"

"Why not?" Hooman challenges her.

"When did theater become so subversive?" asks Leili. "There are a lot of plays . . . every night," she says. "They're fun and have nice music and some even have dancing, sort of."

"Ten years ago, before they knew how to censor it, doing theater *was* subversive. Remember Taheri's *Blacks*? Now it's *not* doing theater that's subversive," Arezoo explains.

"I'm confused," Leili admits.

Hooman says, "That's exactly what the government wants—to silence directors and writers. They allow a lot of loud, energetic, musical distractions to give the impression that they are open-minded."

"And to entertain the public under a pretense that they're getting what they want," Arezoo adds.

"But in all the razzmatazz what gets lost are the words, the essence of what a good play is all about—critique, commentary. Are you guys in?" Hooman asks abruptly.

"Why the rush?" Nima asks.

"Where will you . . . ?" Leili asks.

"We," Hooman corrects her. "Join us?"

"I don't act," Leili says.

"So?"

"When are practices?" Leili asks practically.

Hooman leans toward Leili and forces her to look into his earnest expression. "What's your gut feeling?" he asks.

"My gut feels a little strange. Maybe it was the café glacé."

"Sounds like a yes." He reaches out across the table and covers her hand with his own.

"I'm really out of shape," Leili responds.

"You're fine," Arezoo says curtly.

"We're all going to get into shape together, starting with some tai chi."

"Sounds yummy," Arezoo says.

"It's an ancient Chinese exercise," Hooman says. He hands them each a slip of paper. "Address is on the back, see you next week, same time."

بسم الله الرحمن الرحيم

In the Name of God

Leili's wrists are thin like the legs of a sparrow: tough but delicate.

Am I asking too much of her, of all of them? An actor needs courage . . . not just to go on stage but what Grotowski calls a "passive courage . . . the courage of the defenseless, the courage to reveal oneself."

Don't think we'll be doing much revealing anytime soon, unless, of course, we want to cause a riot. I probably shouldn't be keeping a journal of the project, but if I don't, it's like our little experiment never happened—who would know? The Komiteh, for one. I'd be giving them more evidence if they found it. First they'd have to translate it. I'm writing some of it in English. Makes it easier, too, when people in cafés try to peek over my shoulder. I should call it Notes Underground, *or* Notes from the Underground *or maybe just* Director's Notes *or simply* Journal. *I'll try to keep my personal thoughts to myself, keep to the theme of our project . . . might be hard.*

Risk: is it cultural? Generational? Personality? Deviant? Is it just a word? Was it really risky of Arezoo to write a message on a wall? Was it riskier for me to answer it and audition? It would be now, but it wasn't so much back then. Khatami was president and the world was our oyster. Before him, talking to a girl in public, listening to music, doing theater were all risks—haram, not sanctioned by religion. We couldn't even sit in a café together without the Komiteh barging in and breaking it up, asking for IDs to make sure we were married, siblings or cousins.

His presidency was an odd moment of openness—a total anomaly in a thirty-year span. On a life-graph it would look like a little explosion of energy with a flat line before and after. Flatlining: dead. We flatlined after Khatami left and now I'm determined to perform some resuscitation. Call it a risk, or call it a play.

October 1st
Leili asked why we are hiding if the City Theater is open. We're going to do something other than just theater: something radical. Our play will take place simultaneously with other plays going on above board—overhead, so to speak. And maybe that's the real issue; life out there looks better than it actually is. It's all about keeping up appearances, because really, things are worse than ever. If it didn't at least appear normal we'd all protest. It would be much more honest for the government to shut down everyone's performances and admit that it's all censored than allow some plays to be produced just to give the impression that there is an open, uncensored theater—which is not the case.

Nima thinks it doesn't matter as long as we are able to entertain ourselves, he's satisfied with enough. He doesn't understand this drive, call it artistic, intellectual, political . . . but I want to do more, to be able to say more.

My play will use banned texts and banned bodies and banned minds and courageous actors. Which is why Leili's risky outburst caught my attention in class. And then she just happened to walk by, alone. I don't believe in coincidences.

Arcadia

A block away from the theater is a narrow alley that leads to the old calligrapher's arcade. It is exactly as Hooman has described it on the slip of paper: two alleys back and a gutter deep. The actual abandoned arcade is a deserted four-story skeleton of derelict, dirty, dark balconied shop stalls built to look inward—like a Paris arcade bombed in the war.

"No windows," Leili mutters to herself. Once inside it could either provide the perfect protection—or be hiding the worst kind of danger. Leili looks around, wishing she owned a cellphone or even a whistle—some way to call for help once she's inside.

She takes a deep breath and pushes the heavy metal door. It squeaks open to a shaft of warm sunlight. The other side of the building is lined in windows and completely exposed to the boulevard. The center of the arcade, a tin skeleton of dangling glass shards spattered in pigeon poop, provides little shelter.

"Hooman?" Leili calls tentatively into the musty expanse. "Hooman!" she shouts when he doesn't reply.

"Shhh," Nima answers, coming around a corner. "Over here."

She steps over a mound of trash. "Sorry, I didn't see you. Where is he?"

"Late."

They stand tentatively, each eyeing the windows in the long hallway at the foot of the stairs.

"We shouldn't be here. We could get in big trouble for trespassing. For being . . ."

"I know," Nima cuts her off.

"Up here!" calls Arezoo. They look up at the landing where Arezoo stands in the light and litter.

"It's too dangerous down there. That long hallway of windows exposes you to the street. Come up, quick," she instructs them.

"Where's Hooman?" Nima wants to know.

"Checking out the roof. All's clear; follow me and I'll take you there," Arezoo says.

Like an overgrown vine searching for light, the staircase weaves its way through the center of the building to the hidden top floor. Along the way, like an archeology of detritus, layers of the building's history unfold underfoot: filmy tape from old cassettes strewn about loosely after the music store closed shop, hundreds of unused white cardboard pastry boxes that Arezoo kicks to part the way and musty and moldy magazines from the news sellers.

"Perfect," Nima agrees when they arrive at the sunlit and high-walled roof.

Hooman waves them over to where he is crouched down on the floor studying a very large book.

"Last week I found this old Chinese tai chi manual. Check it out."

Faded pen-and-ink drawings show a dance of sprightly animals. Heavy bamboo brushstrokes create movement in stillness.

"Beautiful," Leili comments over Hooman's shoulder.

Hooman traces his fingers across the dusty pages. "Imagine us turning our arms and coaxing our legs."

"Dancing through dust." Arezoo bends down and wipes her finger across the dusty page.

Hooman stands and says, "Get in a line."

"Where's the other guy?" Nima asks Arezoo, looking around the empty rooftop for emphasis.

"He's busy; he'll come soon. He's very famous . . ."

"OK," Hooman interrupts. "Line up."

Their backs to the door, Leili, Hooman, Arezoo and Nima face the street wall.

"Arms up." Hooman demonstrates The Bear. "Breathe in . . . let your arms go; slap them about like wet noodles . . ."

From Flying Wild Goose to Lioness on Alert and some ten animals in between, they finally end the long qi gong and tai chi practice and come to a place of stillness.

"We'll close with a meditation," Hooman tells them. "In tai chi, we stand to meditate in the Wu Chi position, knees slightly bent, wrists slightly curved . . ."

They are barely settled into the Wu Chi position when there's a sudden bang. They all turn at once to see the roof door slam shut behind four bearded teenagers dressed like Basij in white button-down oxfords and black pants who come pummeling at them.

"Run!" yells Hooman, grabbing Leili and swerving past the flock of vigilantes. Arezoo holds the door while Nima pushes one of the boys away. Hooman reaches into his bag and throws a paperback across the roof. The men all run toward the book while the four friends flee via the stairwell.

Outside, Nima doubles over. "I'm out of shape."

"Shit," Arezoo says, "I hear them."

"Let's split up and meet at Naderi," Hooman says. "Go."

Leili, who is easy to lose in a crowd thanks to the same non-descript rupush and *magna'eh* that all the other young women in the university district wear, follows behind Hooman at a clipped but steady pace. They walk up Revolution Street, past the City

Theater and then the textbook sellers and secret underground publishing presses, toward Vali Asr, Tehran's little Champs-Élysées where sycamore trees already wear their deepest autumnal red, into and then out of the gates of Amir Kabir University and across to Villa, the old Armenian district lined with handicraft stores and Danish pastry shops.

"Over here," Leili calls from behind Hooman.

Hooman turns to find her pointing toward the Armenian Cathedral on the corner of Villa.

"They won't look for us in here," she says.

"But I . . ."

"It's OK."

The church is dark and smells of incense.

"It's vacant. Who's guarding it?" Hooman asks.

"The angels," Leili says, still catching her breath. She directs him to a pew.

"Are you . . . ?"

"Christian" says Leili, quickly changing the subject. "Why were they chasing us? It's not like they could really do anything. And why were we taking it so seriously?"

"They wanted to make sure we got the idea to never go back in there."

"No problem!"

"Come on, the others are probably already at Naderi." Hooman stands up abruptly, clearly uncomfortable in the church.

"Any other brilliant meeting spots, Hooman?" Nima asks as they join him at a table in the far corner of the café.

"As a matter of fact, yes." Hooman says.

"Where?" asks Nima, raising his eyebrows at Arezoo.

"The City Theater," Hooman answers. Arezoo laughs.

Nima chuckles. "Seriously."

"An American embassy will be rebuilt before we're ever allowed into that place again," Arezoo jokes.

"We don't need a theater, Hooman. You always told us that the audience was secondary to our own experience," Nima reminds him.

"This time is different. We'll still work really hard in practice, but the performance is our main goal. We want to include the audience. We need to wake folks up," Hooman whispers.

Leili shudders. Hooman turns to her and says, "An actor must feel as comfortable walking on to a stage on his hands as on his feet."

Nima exhales and asks, "So where are we rehearsing?"

"Remember the janitor, Agha Mashti, at the university theater?"

"Yeah, he loved us. Brought us tea all the time and watched us practice," says Arezoo.

"Exactly, that guy. I passed him on the street near the City Theater yesterday. He was ecstatic to see me; seems like he's reminded of us often." Hooman winks at Nima. "One of us sent the old man gifts of tea, sugar and a wool sweater last winter."

"He liked it?" Nima asks.

"Enough to tell me about his new job at the City Theater and about a secret theater in the basement there that no one else knows about."

"Someone must know about it."

"He claims that it was used as a storage space after the Revolution, but there was a leaky pipe that destroyed everything in it and now it's a forgotten room. Anyway," Hooman reports, "It's ours if we want it."

"Are you serious?"

"He took me to take a peek. It's a bit messy. We'll have to spend a few days cleaning. We can't know if it's soundproof, but it is well hidden. There's only one way in and out through a door that leads down from the street. It's like a trapdoor hidden in the ground. He gave me the key. What do you say?"

"I'd say *trap* is the operative word," Nima says.

"Really, Hooman. It's right in the center of everything. It's not only directly beneath the City Theater but it's also just shy of the most-watched intersection in Tehran," Arezoo adds.

"Home of the Revolution," Hooman says with a grin.

"That area gets more young pedestrian traffic than anywhere in the city, especially now during the school year. Buf Pizza, the juice spot, Chahar Meez, not to mention the Theater Café, are always packed," says Nima.

"The Basij, the Komiteh, Gasht-e Ershad are crawling in this area." Arezoo states the obvious.

"They won't think to look for us right under their noses," Hooman says calmly.

"Imagine the punishment: women and men, caught together in an enclosed space," Leili says.

"Sweating and touching," Arezoo adds. Leili blushes.

"Not to mention squatting in a government building. God knows what they'd do to us," Nima says. Leili nods emphatically. Arezoo turns to Hooman and asks, "Hooman, could we talk alone for a minute?"

"Anything you want to say to me you can say to the group," Hooman replies.

"You're tired, stressed. Maybe we should make this decision after you've rested," Arezoo says, watching Leili as she speaks. "It's a huge risk, especially for you," Arezoo adds.

Hooman's steely expression says it's the subterranean spot or nothing.

"Maybe it's the perfect spot," Leili offers. "Like chadors that cover illegal satellite dishes on the rooftops, or men with religious-looking beards." She and Hooman exchange smiles. "A foil."

Arezoo catches the exchange and quickly interjects, "Hooman,

it's all great, except for the space." She sighs, "I'll ask around."
Arezoo gets up to leave when Leili says, "I'm in."

Arezoo sits back down in her chair and glares at Leili. "I'll
look at the space," she says curtly.

"Bring work clothes with you," says Hooman. "We have to go
in one at a time so as not to attract attention. And I don't have to
tell you about the danger involved."

"It's near the fountain, isn't it?" Nima asks.

"Yes."

"Shall we meet there?"

"Thursday night."

"Thursday? You're crazy! It's the busiest night of the week.
It's opening night at the City Theater," Arezoo warns them.

"And therefore the loudest night, and the day that the theater
administrative offices are officially closed," Hooman says.

"OK," says Nima. He and Hooman quickly stand. Arezoo
throws an air kiss at them as they go.

"Wait." Arezoo puts a hand on Leili as she stands to leave.
"You should know what you're getting yourself into."

"What do you mean?" asks Leili. She sits back down on the
edge of her seat and watches the men leave.

"We weren't just reprimanded by heathen censors the last
time we tried to put on a play. Our practice space at school was
stormed by the Basij." Arezoo continues: "Hooman hit a nerve
with them. They shoved him against the wall and called him a
traitor to the Islamic Republic."

Leili flinches.

"They said something about a merciful warning for one who
should know better. Then they warned him that they had a special cell in Evin for traitors. They kept him for a night." Arezoo
pauses, then asks: "Ever been to Evin? Visit a family member,
maybe?"

Leili shakes her head faintly.

"It's a scary place. Built right into the side of a mountain for maximum security."

"Yes," Leili replies softly. Everyone who lives in Tehran knows where Evin is. Anyone who has been on a weekend hike to Darakeh or gone there to eat liver and heart kabobs on the weekend has passed by Evin.

"When was this?" Leili whispers.

"Not so long ago, maybe six months back, just before I graduated. They stormed his dorm room, took most of his books. Hooman was put on probation and expelled from the dorms. He fell into a bad depression. I thought he was done with theater for sure."

"Oh," Leili says.

Arezoo stands and says, "Don't get me wrong, I love the theater. I loved our group and I'm happy he's feeling better and . . . inspired." She waits, and when Leili doesn't comment, she adds, "You should know that this is a huge risk."

بسم الله الرحمن الرحيم

In the Name of God

As we walked back to Naderi together today, Leili told me that when she
was a child her father took a risk that didn't end well. I can just imagine
it as a scene in a play.

Overcast and bitterly cold day.

Leili's little feet felt like blocks of ice as she and her father rushed
through their errands. They were just making their way to the baker
when they ran into a War Remembrance parade. Women dressed from
head to toe in black chadors and men in white sheets streaked with red
paint (bloody shrouds) chanted: "Paradise can only be reached by martyrdom. Martyrdom is not death but a new life."

Her father taught photography and always had his faithful Brownie
camera with him. He snapped the lens cap off as quickly as he could and
began to shoot away.

The incriminating flash of light and sound of the clicking haunts her
still: click click, click, unknowingly in rhythm with the Komiteh officer's
boots hitting the pavement behind them. A bushy-bearded man with eyes
hidden behind sunglasses on that sunless day fumbled his prayer beads
as he approached them. If only she had known then that such a simple,
frightening gesture would become so commonplace now, such a routine
interaction in the streets of Tehran: a plainclothed Komiteh placing his
prayer beads in his pocket in order to use both hands to reprimand and
take his prey. Scary? No: status quo.

She wasn't afraid at first. It looked like a difference of opinion between
two men in the street, like the time her dad had a little fender bender

and the drivers got out of their cars, had a brief but explosive argument, and ended with a double-cheek kiss and a return to their cars. This man wasn't about to settle for a double-cheek kiss. These days he would settle for a bribe, but back then, as the war ended, Revolutionary fervor was high and ideals were more valuable than money.

"ID," he demanded.

Beads of sweat covered her father's forehead, frown-lines replaced his dimples, his mouth was drawn and his lips pursed. My grandmother used to say, "Don't make ugly faces. Your face might freeze in that position." And his had.

That day Leili learned that words, too, freeze mid-air when they are thrown out carelessly. Words can seep into the crease of a forehead, settle into a hidden dimple, and fall darkly between the brows.

When they returned home, her father's hands were still shaking — apparently they never stopped — and he abandoned photography forever. After that day everything came out blurry, including Leili's memories, which became coated with a layer of hope — of delusion.

The smell of sautéed garlic and eggplant that they would not eat greeted them from the kitchen. The smell of bergamot above all else gave her every sense of the safety of home despite a deep and unfamiliar silence.

They walked into the kitchen where she expected her mother to turn around, smile, hug them and pour tea. But instead her face was buried in her hands. She was sobbing. (I wonder what she looks like? If she's delicate and beautiful like her daughter? Date-colored eyes, orange and brown?)

"Someone came?" her father asked. (Leili tells me he was very handsome, with dark hair and light skin like hers). Leili looked at her mother, confused.

"Called." Her mother looked up. She looked at Leili and wiped her tears. "We can discuss this later. Come, eat."

"I'm not hungry," her father said. His appetite never did return (I'm guessing, because Leili says he never eats).

Later, when her parents thought she was fast asleep, Leili listened, and observed how words like photographs have form and are sculptural;

have speed when in motion—how they stay in the mind long after the eyes shut.

Her mother told her father that a man had called and that he was to report to the local Komiteh first thing in the morning. Her mother's words vibrated like an out-of-control cord. The cord broke that night; words have limits. (We could pull a string along the stage; it could vibrate as it separates her parents on either side).

The next night Leili found her mother, Saqi (great name—pourer of wine), standing in the kitchen crying; her apron was a mess of olive oil and flour and her face had changed that night. It has since been softened by time, like a fossil that hardens its core but loses its edges.

Her father had reported to the Komiteh. He was accused of illegal photography. They took his best camera and forbade him to teach— purged him from his university position.

"But I marched for the Revolution," he cried as they escorted him out.

(Imagine him leaning forward, practically coming out of his cool brown leather Dracula-lapelled jacket as they hold his arms back by the sleeves.)

Not going to work led to not leaving the house. Leili mistook her mother's extra effort to do her husband's share as compassion, but she was simply being practical. She ran the errands and the household and grew an invisible barrier—a line that her father rarely crossed. (I'm exaggerating, but isn't that what drama's all about? Or is that melodrama?)

Leili tells me her father is jovial and kind. She also told me that he gave her his camera recently. I asked if the sound of clicking still bothers her. She laughed and so I suggested a series of photographs of the city to use as a backdrop. Nima's cousin owns a printing shop. He can get a deal and we can hang them on stage . . . First we need a place to hang them from. A safe place to hang . . . (out, from, in).

Day Turns Black

Leili takes a long, deep breath and darts across the motionless rush-hour traffic where at the first opportunity an engine will gun forward dangerously and without warning. Cars are the least of her worries as she walks toward the theater complex, a large octagonal performance building where people are already in line at the ticket booth in the front and at the other five side doors that lead to the three main auditoriums and the café. The cement benches that circle the building are packed with waiting theatergoers and families who have stopped to listen to the street performers drawing crowds to the plaza of the theater—an old man playing the accordion and another man farther in playing the violin. Leili pauses to listen to the violinist, who plays her favorite song, a forties ballad called "Sultan of the Heart." The plaza-and-theater complex is flanked by bustling Vali Asr Avenue on one side and a park on the other and feeds out into a vital transit hub: there are a metro stop, a bus depot and four taxi stands within a block of the theater. The whole complex is the centerpiece of the wildly popular university district made up of Tehran University (a concrete Nazi-built hall that looks more like a government office than a university, where in 1979 the Iranian Revolution came to fruition) and across the street, Amir Kabir University and next to it the Faculty of Fine Art. Between them are bookstores, cafés, cinemas and various institutes, from dentistry to philosophy.

Leili turns left toward the park and heads to the fountain, which is rumored to be risky after sunset—a meeting place for pimps and pushers.

Pale blue tiles refract the light of the setting sun and create a halo of silver around the fountain. She perches on the edge of the fountain at the northwest corner and places her backpack between her legs. The faint sound of the violin joins a reassuring hum of people nearby. The city takes her inside the fold of its black chador and wraps her into the anonymity of the dark night, where she sits unseen and watches families, day workers and students slowly wind their way home along the path that passes by the fountain. One by one, the night workers—Afghan trash collectors, pimps, dealers and dapper young men—materialize from the dark. The fountain area turns from neutral to male in minutes. Leili picks up her backpack and hugs it to her chest. It's soon obvious that none of these men are interested in Leili or her possessions, especially not the teenage boy in a tight mustard-colored polyester shirt and purple pants who casually strolls past her in search of another young man to wander off with toward the public restroom.

Leili looks away politely and sees another figure emerge from the shadows. She catches her breath. It's as if a famous film actor has just walked off the screen. He comes toward her and she wishes she had worn a nicer rupush, something more colorful and sleek. He wears a white t-shirt under a black denim jacket, tight black jeans and matching Chuck Taylor sneakers. He pauses at the fountain near Leili and lights a cigarette. He takes a long shaky drag.

"You must be waiting for Hooman," he says.

Leili nods. "You too?" she asks, touching her hot cheek.

"Kamran," he says unnecessarily. He fishes a thread of loose tobacco off his tongue and makes a sour face.

"Scary?" Leili offers.

"What?" he asks without looking at her, his gaze on the boys in the shadows.

"This theater idea."

"Oh." He flicks his honey-brown chin-length hair and drags on his cigarette. Smoke comes out of his tiny button nose that everyone in Tehran knows was reconstructed. His fingers tap his cigarette pack. His infamous jade-green eyes dart here and there, on alert—he tries to take measured drags on his cigarette and act cool, but he's not the best actor.

Arezoo, dressed in anything but cleaning clothes, suddenly appears before them in a scarlet scarf, black cape and lips lined in plum and filled in dark purple lipstick. She ignores Leili and beams broadly at Kamran.

"I jumped into a Peykan thinking it was a cab. When I asked to get out, the guy said, 'Ms., I have a masters degree, I'm not driving a cab.' The poor SOB thought I was out there working the streets. It's exhausting," she says with a sigh.

"But you made it," Kamran remarks and takes another tight drag on his cigarette.

"What a pity that you've been banned over something so silly," Arezoo says, still catching her breath, still ignoring Leili.

"Yes, I shouldn't have shown my face at Cannes last year, not with her, anyway."

"Poor woman," Leili says.

"Why?" asks Kamran, turning to her. "She had a wonderful career in Iran. If she's dumb enough to think that posing nude for a European magazine wouldn't get her in trouble then she deserves what she got." Kamran pauses briefly, then adds, "Besides, it's not like she's been punished; she got away. She's free, living it up in Europe. I'm the one who's stuck here, blacklisted from working after making that silly film with her."

"Sorry," Leili mutters.

"It's definitely to our advantage," Arezoo purrs.

"What choice do I have with all the good film directors either under house arrest or working abroad?"

Hooman and Nima arrive dressed in old jeans and flannels. Hooman gives Kamran a quick handshake and says "Welcome."

Kamran sighs dramatically. "Got to keep the machine oiled."

"Gutsy," Arezoo approves.

Leili looks at Arezoo. "Banned?" she whispers.

"Stage and screen. He's a risk for sure," Arezoo smiles sweetly.

Kamran laughs. "Now, let's not be dramatic."

"Nima will escort you to the entrance area," Hooman says curtly. He turns toward the fountain and lights a cigarette.

The "entrance" is a gunnysack construction curtain that they wait behind like children lined up in the schoolyard on the first day of class.

They stand shoulder to shoulder against a cold concrete wall gazing into the dark musty expanse and holding their breath until Hooman appears and lights a small handheld lantern—the kind Leili's mother still uses at home during electricity blackouts. The light reveals a twist of concrete stairs leading down into what could be a catacomb.

They all begin to move at once. "Slowly," Hooman warns them. "Single-file," he says, "it's a deep descent."

The cement stairs spiral down like a Chinese fan that opens into a deep cylindrical space.

"It's damp." Nima is the first to speak when they land in the cold, dark oval-shaped room.

Leili looks around at the floor-to-ceiling cement. "It feels like a mausoleum," she whispers. Goosebumps prickle her skin.

Everything, including benches that are built right into the walls, is cement. Barely discernable patches of light gray on the sooty black diesel-streaked walls suggest that the janitor, Mashti, has attempted and failed to clean the space for them. Piles of pre-Revolution playbills, the pages unreadable and stuck together from years of flooding and drying until they became unreadable bricks and musty velvet cushions that must have once lined the cement seats lie around in heavy, unmovable heaps. Nima sneezes.

"Shhh."

Leili hears a drip, but the light is too dim to find its source. She wonders if stalactites have begun to form slowly below whatever unseen hole is releasing constant, tiny tears.

"There's a small airhole in the ceiling," Hooman says, as if reading her mind.

"Small for sure. The smell of diesel and urine hasn't found it," Nima says, holding a Kleenex to his nose.

According to Mashti, after the Revolution the small theater became a diesel gas storage room before it was "cleaned" for reuse. Whatever use that may have been is not clearly marked in the remains they have before them: gum wrappers, plastic slippers, four antique Singer sewing tables and kitschy posters of Imam Hussein crisscrossed with tape that is peeling off like an old Band-Aid from a fresh scab.

"Guess we'll have to incorporate all these things as props. There's no way that we can take them out without being seen," says Nima. Hooman makes no comment, but it's obvious from the way he looks at the trash and then at the stairs that he disagrees.

"It's so absurd," Kamran jokes. When no one laughs he explains, "It was built during the Shah's time for theater of the absurd. The Queen had it built for her avant-garde theater buddies."

"Ionesco, Genet. It's about the breakdown of language, of reason," Arezoo adds.

"Perfect for Iran," Nima says. "Can't censor mumbo jumbo."

"You'd be surprised," Kamran remarks.

"It's whatever we make of it," Hooman says. He takes his canvas backpack off and dumps the contents on the ground: rags, rubber gloves, detergent, a small straw broom, razors, alcohol, bleach, electrical tape and a Swiss Army knife.

"We're going to make this place our own safe space." He hands Nima the small hand broom.

"I . . ." Arezoo clears her throat as if to make an announcement.

"Shhh," Hooman warns her. "We're not sure how soundproof this place is so limit your chatter." He hands her and Leili the detergent and rags. "Mashti left buckets and some water here somewhere."

"Sir?" Kamran bows with his arms out, ready to receive.

Hooman hands him a razor. "Start with whatever that gunk is on the back wall," he tells him. Kamran wrinkles his little nose but turns toward the wall, razor in hand.

"I'm going back upstairs for more water from Mashti," Hooman says and throws a second rag to Arezoo, who gingerly folds it in fours. She waits for direction, standing perfectly straight, as if already on stage. Hooman turns without further instruction and ascends the stairs.

"Hooman, the light," Nima's voice is throaty and urgent underground.

Hooman walks back down. "Sorry." He hands Nima a match and a small emergency candle. He walks partway up the stairs and as he rounds the bend, the theater falls into darkness.

He calls down to Leili: "Leili, come with me and take the light back down. We only have this one. I'll come back down and get you."

"Wait." Her voice is urgent. "Just a minute.

"What is it?" Hooman asks.

"It's . . . amazing. I had no idea things could get so dark."

"Too young to remember the war?" Arezoo remarks.

Nima frowns at her in the dark.

"Come on." Hooman appears with the light and takes Leili's elbow.

"What's so amazing about the dark, anyway?" he asks her as they climb shoulder to shoulder up the narrow stairs.

"Its completeness, its anonymity, its depth," she whispers.

"That's a very philosophical answer for a ten-second experience."

"Do profound experiences need a long time?" Leili asks.

"No."

"The dark doesn't make you just a little on edge, or excited?" Leili coaxes.

"Maybe a little scared, a little on my toes. I like that I can't see where I begin or end."

Leili smiles to the dark.

To the average pedestrian walking through the theater compound, their roof, just behind the main building on the park side, appears to be an innocuous waist-level adobe mound with a barely visible peephole—like a nipple on a breast. Apart from the occasional joint smoker, few people walk behind the theater. Had Mashti not pointed it out, Hooman would not have known where to lean over and look down.

"Even if we completely lit the theater below, with all the city's light pollution a passerby would hardly notice it," he tells Leili.

He leans over and projects his voice down into the fourteen-foot depth. Either no one answers or he cannot hear the reply over the hustle and bustle of the city.

"I'll check again later," he whispers to Leili. "The area stays loud until about eleven o'clock, but I foresee even later nights."

"Really?"

"Really."

Down below, Leili follows Hooman with the dim lantern as he splashes soapy water in each corner.

Kamran, crossed-legged, smokes and stares into space. Hooman takes his scrub cloth and wrings it out for him and hands it back. "Here, you need to scrub with more vigor. Where's the razor?" Kamran points to Arezoo. "We traded," he says.

Leili carefully piles garbage in her corner with only an occasional glance at the accumulated debris. She studies Arezoo, who scrapes away at the walls intently, glancing every now and then at Hooman.

She feels faint from the diesel fumes, the acrid intensity of the bleach and the dust awakened from sleep by Nima's sweeping. Arezoo stands dramatically and unveils her short, sleek black bob. Without a word or any comments from the others, who pretend that they aren't watching her out of the corner of their eyes, she ties her scarf around her mouth like a bandit and returns to her task.

Hooman glances at Leili, who readjusts her plastic gloves and rearranges her little rubbish heap in response. She picks up a dirty little black plastic bag—the kind that string beans are sold in—and stifles a scream.

Hooman runs to her. "What happened?"

She points to the bag, stretched with use and age, and her face sours.

"Inside," she says, careful not to touch it.

"Dead rat?" He asks. The gutters downtown are full of them.

"No," she whispers. She takes off her rubber gloves and throws them on the floor.

The group gathers around as Hooman crouches down and gingerly opens the offending bag of used hypodermic needles.

"Addicts," Kamran whispers nonchalantly.

Leili listens to the casual conversation about whether the needles are old or new, about the soaring HIV rate, whether the needles were in use here or dropped through the hole in the ceiling and wonders if she's the only one who has never seen drug paraphernalia.

"Mashti must have . . . ," Nima begins to say.

"Shhh," Hooman interrupts. Hooman swiftly sweeps the offending mess into a dustpan and dumps it into the collective trash bag. He brushes off his shaking hands on his pants and says, "Back to work."

Leili doesn't move. She stands with her gloves off as everyone else returns to their work.

The others scrub away diligently in their corners, careful not to look in her direction, save Nima, who turns toward her and moves slightly as if to go to her. Hooman motions for him to wait.

Arezoo crawls past Nima like an alley cat that owns the street and whispers, "Our pretty, innocent little engineer is going to need more dedication than a schoolgirl crush."

"This dedicated engineer is going back to work," Nima answers, "And so should you."

Kamran lights a cigarette. Hooman inhales the second-hand smoke and holds his breath before telling him, "Put it out."

Hooman watches Leili, who bites her fingernails and stares at the dust that dances in the dim light. She suddenly steps forward and Hooman says, "Wait, don't move." His hand springs up like a stop sign. He motions for Arezoo to follow him over to Leili.

"You looked just like a Rodin sculpture I once saw."

Arezoo raises her eyebrows at Hooman.

"In a banned art book," he explains. "The sculpture was stepping forward and leaning toward an anticipated direction, but was sculpted forever into the moment before movement. It's the perfect pose to open our play with."

Nima joins them with a sketchbook and studies Leili. He jots down notes and makes little sketches.

"Don't move," Hooman repeats when Leili turns to look at Nima's sketch. "Trust me, he's quite good—he's our official stage blocker."

Leili holds her breath as they move around her. "See the way her jaw muscles ripple, the inflection of her neck tendons, the delicate way her wrist just hangs," Hooman points out.

Leili sways. "I can't breathe," she whispers.

Nima takes one of her wet and clammy hands to steady her.

"They're just needles," Arezoo tells her. But Leili isn't listening. She has closed her eyes.

"Back off, don't crowd her. It's the air down here; she just needs some good, dirty Tehran air," Hooman says. He puts his arm underneath her shoulder and signals for Nima to do the same.

They seat her gently on the landing behind the curtain.

"OK?" Hooman asks.

Leili nods and he leaves.

"Better?" Nima asks.

"Yeah."

"See you down there," he says confidently and turns to leave.

"Nima," Leili calls him back. "Is it true that the Basij stormed your last play?"

"Yes," he whispers. He leaves without elaborating.

A light drizzle turns to slow, staccato drips. Gaudy and bright neon makes Tehran look like a woman dressed in sequins, smudged lipstick and runny mascara—she should be covered. Leili watches the blur of people walk aimlessly through the night. Her breath and pulse slowly return to normal as she stares into the dark nothingness and enjoys the reprieve from having to think, worry, move, do and wonder. Tonight she can be still.

She hugs her legs to her chest and rests her chin on her knees. She closes her eyes and relives the warmth and care with which Nima and Hooman brought her up the stairs. She stands up, takes a long deep breath of air and turns to feel for the first step. One careful step at a time, she descends back into the dark.

بسم الله الرحمن الرحيم

In the Name of God

Finished translating a chunk of Grotowski, my buddy, Agha, Mr. Jerzy. Sometimes, I worry that I'm wasting my time on some obscure crazy person, but then there aren't a lot of other theater handbooks hanging out in the backroom booksellers and every time I translate something he wrote, I'm even more convinced that he is speaking directly to me. Listen to this: Agha Jerzy says

> *The rhythm of life in modern civilization is characterized by pace, tension, a feeling of doom, the wish to hide our personal motives and the assumption of a variety of roles and masks in life . . . we try to divide ourselves artificially into body and soul. When we try to liberate ourselves from it all we start to shout and stamp, we convulse to the rhythm of music.*

What I like about him is that he understood the pain of not being allowed to use our God-given gifts—such as, say, a talent for provocation. He began the Polish Laboratory Theater in the late fifties (Stalin's time—so we have a few things in common). Texts and performances were censored but rehearsals went undetected. Rehearsals are where it all happened—magic between two or three human beings that was untouched by the outside. The Polish Lab used rigorous exercises to teach the actors full control of their bodies. He wanted an actor to use her body and voice without makeup and costumes and lighting—even text. I like this. He was against shame (guess he wasn't too into religion). He says

> *Neither that which touches the interior sphere nor the profound stripping bare of the self should be regarded as evil so long as in the process . . . they produce an act of creation . . . reveal and purify us while we transcend ourselves. Indeed, they improve us then.*

> *I hope this will be an improvement. I know it will be regarded as evil by some pious keepers of the faith, and I know that I shouldn't really write this but if I don't I may forget the nuances of it . . . of the fear that sometimes creeps over me, like now. I'm scared.*

Enough. Reading, translating, thinking . . . at least for tonight. I have enough to begin the exercises. Tomorrow is a big day. It will change things. It will make the theater more physical, more political, more meaningful—more dangerous. I hope they'll agree to do these moves, to touch. We reach a turning point thus: will they reveal or continue to conceal, and what will either act ultimately lead to? The show must go on . . .

Traffic

Leili's parents are perched against the big *poshties* in her father's library watching Saqi's favorite Tehran sitcom, "The Beautiful Barbershop," when Leili walks in the door three hours later than she said she'd be home.

Saqi looks up, opens her mouth to speak, catches herself and smiles instead. Her father takes a sip from his glass tumbler and acknowledges her with a nod without taking his eyes off the screen.

"Reruns, come sit," Saqi says.

Leili stands in the doorway and watches the end of the show, most of which takes place with the characters stuck in a Tehran traffic jam. The characters flirt across a freeway, windows down, horns honking and jumping in and out of each other's cars for sport.

"It's so silly," Leili comments. "Tehran's never that fun. If it were a documentary people would be sitting in their cars complaining to the camera about how difficult it is to get around this city."

"That's why we watch fiction and not the news." Saqi's reply is cheerful.

"Most people just sit and wait for life to happen," Leili comments.

"Don't be so gloomy; it's fun."

"What, the traffic?"

"Is that why you're late? Traffic?" Her father is curt.

Leili doesn't answer; she's sure she's not meant to. Her father isn't really paying attention once the tumbler appears.

"Leili, you're tired? I don't blame you—the streets are crazy," Saqi soothes. "Come sit with us." She scoots over and pats the cushion between herself and her husband.

"Sometimes in the streets, despite all the hustle and bustle of the city, if you just stop for a minute and look, which no one ever really does, you'll find that no one is really moving at all but rather expending needless energy moving in place," Leili says.

"True." Saqi gives Leili a worried look. She pats the seat again and Leili sits down carefully on the poshti. Saqi, without taking her eyes off the television, gives Leili a little hug.

Leili watches, imagining people toning future muscles, watching, preparing and passing time until an opportunity presents itself to banish the inertia, to make a change and leap forward. She wonders which of them is waiting for the future and which are just waiting out the present.

The show ends and her father starts his nightly channel surfing, back and forth between the only three channels on Islamic Republic of Iran broadcasting. He's too cheap to splurge on a satellite dish.

"Better?" Saqi asks Leili.

"Just tired," Leili replies, rubbing her legs that are sore from the long rehearsal.

Her father flips to a war documentary of smiling young soldiers with longish hair and sneakers who pass under and kiss a Koran before going off to battle. He immediately flips the channel back to the Muzak Mullah station.

"Wait," Leili protests as he changes the channel. "Go back."

"Garbage. We saw enough of this propaganda during the war."

"I'm curious," Leili says.

"Really?" Saqi is surprised.

Her father stays stubbornly on the image of a schoolgirl placing flowers around Khomeini's grave.

"Aren't you at all curious?" Leili asks.

"About what?" Saqi asks.

"We lost an entire generation of young boys who should be raising children now. Ten years of needless fighting. We all came out losers in that war," her father informs her, and adds, "What more is there to know?"

"Nothing," Leili mutters.

"Why this sudden interest in the war?" Saqi's voice is gentle.

"I have some reading for class," Leili says and gets up to leave. Her father barely nods as she leaves; Saqi scoots over and stretches her legs over where Leili was sitting.

بسم الله الرحمن الرحيم

In the Name of God

A dynamic disquiet? All this theory, all these thoughts, working through all this English is like following a trail of pretty, broken objects. I chase these fragments in a game of hide-and-seek, combing a foreign psychic landscape for pieces of frosted glass that found, still remain just fragments, beautiful in their broken state, but indecipherable—the history of their former shape and culture lost forever. Our broken edges remain sharp. Time has not softened whatever it is that has caused our philosophy to lose its form.

It's as if the ghosts of writers past are lightly tapping on my shoulder. Today's ghost is Ferdowsi: he's come to warn me not to get too close to Zahhak, the ancient Persian prince who was kissed on each shoulder by an evil spirit, after which a serpent sprouted on each side. The spirit advised him to feed the serpents the brain of a youth every day. Sacrificing the intellect and thoughts of the younger generation is an ancient story, one that's ironically banned . . . I could write a modern version of a story like Zahhak.

Friday night . . .
The play comes to me in bits and pieces like these tiny, pretty, shiny objects. I collect and jot down vague descriptions, the contours and the poetry for which I wait patiently—sometimes for hours—to emerge.

A serpent wound around a lovely neck . . . Can't show lovely necks.

I find myself wanting to ask Leili her opinion, but then I stop, afraid to break the spell, afraid of what she might say—and so I avoid her. I watch her reactions closely; I want to know what she thinks of all this. All I see is a good student: determined, earnest and always paying close attention.

Writing is such a lonely act. Some nights the writing is fluid from start to finish. Either way, I remain a medium for illicit ideas to find their way into the realm of the spoken. Other times I'm draped over my bed like a discarded bath towel, too tired and limp to care about continuing. But then something, some sadist muse, keeps insisting.

Above Ground

The café spills outside to the edge of the roof. Tonight the air is crisp and clean and cold, which hardly deters the few regulars, who huddle under heat lamps at the tables scattered across the dark roof.

"Is it warm enough?" Leili asks like a nervous hostess.

"Perfect," Hooman assures her.

"I come here to get out of my house," Leili says too casually.

"What's wrong with your house?" Hooman feigns gravity. "You're an only child, no?"

"Yes, the one and only. It's too quiet. Even at meals."

"Even at meals?" Hooman frowns. "Now that is serious."

"My parents were facing each other at the table, wordless when I left tonight."

Without any effort her father brings silence with him to the table: a silence that mixes with the sizzling onions, the swish of her mother's apron, a faucet that turns on and off, the knife coming down hard on the wood board and her father's labored breathing, amplified in the hollow of the large kitchen where her family eats.

"Meals are the worst."

"I'm sorry," Hooman says gently.

"Don't be; I got out." Mustering a smile, she quickly changes the subject. "What are you reading?"

Hooman pulls a bulky book out of his knapsack: *The Beautiful*

Philosophy of Revolutionary Islam. Leili laughs. "You can't be serious! We've read this a million times."

"And yet somehow, before every exam, I have a knack of forgetting everything I've read in this tome." Hooman shrugs his shoulders.

"That's good. Your mind resists all this crap."

"Crap? Lady, there's a significant difference between coup d'état and revolution. Do you know the difference, Miss?"

"Let me guess: coup d'état is carried out by the oppressor, whereas revolution is carried out by the people."

"Very good!" They laugh.

"Be careful, they'll arrest you for laughing." Hooman lights a cigarette. "I expected to see you in something less conservative up here." He tries to sound casual.

"Why? Because we're in the posh north? Something tight and slinky in red?" she suggests with a laugh. "What makes you think that?"

"Up here everyone tries to get away with less," he muses.

"Who has the energy to keep changing? This way I'm mobile and I'm not forced to be someone I'm not—a miniskirt wearer or a curtain. I'm somewhere in-between permissible and possibility."

"You're still a challenge for the Komiteh. You have so much natural color they must want to wipe something off your face." Hooman blushes slightly and twists the remainder of his cigarette in the ashtray. "What are you reading?" he asks.

"Attar."

"If you submit with grace the Beloved will give his life for you." Hooman whispers a line from Attar, then quickly adds, "Mysticism can be a dangerous interest."

"Why do you say that?"

"Sometimes it's appropriated by the wrong people. Just be careful."

She puts her hands on her lap, leans in over the table, locks eyes with him and lowers her voice. "OK."

"Sorry, I get too serious sometimes."

"Really?" Leili feigns astonishment. Hooman gingerly sips his coffee and lights a cigarette.

"So, tell me about mysticism." He drains his espresso.

She takes a sip of her cappuccino and says, "Ibn Arabi speaks of another world that is only reachable through a different state of consciousness. A dream state by his definition and, centuries later, the unconscious by Freud's."

"Which is it?" Hooman leans in and studies her as she speaks.

"I . . ." She clears her throat, where the intensity of his interest catches.

"Dreams." She begins her tangent, but not before attempting to place her hands on her lap to tame them—to reveal less as she speaks—but then she can't help but lean in closer and place her elbows on the table. She absently plays with a cheap silver ring on her finger.

Hooman leans in. "Interesting ring."

She startles. She had been off somewhere between the subconscious and waking dreams, and he has brought her squarely back into the middle of a smog-choked roof.

She looks down at the ring, twists it off her finger and hands it to him. "I bought it in the bazaar—there's a prayer engraved in it. I can't really read it."

He studies the ring carefully.

"It's a lousy engraving. The letters are so faint. It's too cryptic. I have no idea what it says. Is it from a locksmith at the door of the mosque?" he asks.

"Yes, how did you know?" She's impressed.

"He's the only one in the bazaar who does these kinds of religious rings," he says. "From a soldier friend?"

"A soldier friend?" Leili laughs. "Hardly."

He turns the ring around and examines it between his fingers. "This guy engraved dog tags during the war."

"No wonder it's turning my finger green. I'm afraid to get rid of it, I'm . . ."

"Superstitious." He chuckles and hands back her ring.

"When will we start speaking lines?" Leili asks.

"It's not really about language. It's about the body . . . I mean, the body is . . . , well, it's communicating. Language has boundaries. Even if everyone speaks the same language, it has class inflections, political inflections."

"And the body doesn't?"

Hooman looks up at her and says, "The body's more flexible, more universal in its language. Emotions can be expressed with the body without necessarily politicizing them."

"We are all politicized by virtue of our forced clothing."

"The method we'll use is without costumes or stage sets—it levels the playing field. We are taking the chador off of women and throwing it onto the city—we'll muzzle it. The stage will be empty and black. There are no words—no city screaming at us from its high and mighty walls. We'll use all we have—our ideas, imagination and our bodies. We'll use the very memory in our muscles."

"And you?" Leili gently puts her hand over his to stop him from rolling another cigarette.

"Me?" He pulls his hand back slightly; it shakes.

"What's your muscle memory?"

"One that isn't for theater," he says. He digs into his tobacco pouch. "It's a director's job to act as a medium. I can't muddy the channel with my own emotions." He doesn't look at her.

"What do you do with your emotions?" She asks tentatively, her voice cracks.

"I excavate and exorcise them to a place where they can't hurt anyone," he says quietly. He stands. She looks up, worried.

"I shouldn't have . . . ," she starts.

"Chocolate or lemon poppy seed?" he asks.

She exhales, relieved.

"It's just cake," he says and winks.

Leili watches the candle while she waits for Hooman to return. The light chases and follows the air in a perfect choreography of consumption where movement evolves from need rather than desire. She wonders if the pattern of her breathing is as beautiful, if her breath senses the difference between need and desire. She needs air now, but she won't desire it until it is gone. She puts her finger on the edge of the candle and presses the warm wax as far as it will go. The wax releases her skin unscathed, but not before it has taken an imprint, so perfect, so sharp—as if she has shed a layer of her own skin.

"Like a fossil," she says quietly. She looks up to find a very still Hooman studying her.

"It is the opposite of a fossil. It will be gone tomorrow," he says.

She pushes the candle away and makes room for the large slice of chocolate cake. He hands her a fork and says, "I'll be right back with our coffee."

She digs into the cake.

"We were meant to share that," he says, setting down the cups.

"That was fast."

"What were you thinking about just now? You look so serious." He sits.

"Fireflies," she whispers.

"What are fireflies?"

"Flying beetles with amazing little lights that go on and off to attract mates. They come out in early summer in parts of the world far from here. I did a science report on them in elementary school. Tonight's the kind of night they'd come out."

"Tell them to stay put. The Komiteh doesn't like inner light. They'd be caught in an instant."

"And the whole damn prison would light up. They come from Western Europe and America. Children collect them in jars to make little lanterns. We're like fireflies, forced to hide our light."

"Sounds combustible, no, madame engineer?" He pauses, opens his mouth to add something but stops.

Leili asks, "Why is light so dangerous? In Islam, women's heads are covered because a light emanates from their hair and distracts men. Women are like fireflies."

"So are men," Hooman adds carefully.

"Really, how?"

"In war, for example, the minute a soldier is seen—illuminated—he is as good as dead."

"What do you know about war?" Leili blurts.

"No more than the average Iranian male." Hooman abruptly downs his coffee and crushes his cigarette in the ashtray and packs his things into his backpack.

"Hooman," Leili starts.

He stops her. "It's late. Leili joon, I have to go."

بسم الله الرحمن الرحيم
In the Name of God

November??? Not sure what day it is.

I must be in a good mood, because I love everything I read. Like this — I just read it: Paul Gauguin says that art is either plagiarism or revolution. One will lead to the other — I'm hoping.

"The play's the thing wherein I'll catch the conscience of the king."
— Shakespeare.

I remember when the Basij came to my school to collect a few rogue Shakespeare paperbacks a kid found in the library (turns out no one ever really cleaned the place). It was like they had made some amazing archeological discovery; only the equivalent of a bomb squad rather than archeologists were called in. At least we agree that books are more powerful than bombs.

"Why's he taking them?" we asked our teacher.

"He writes about kings and imperialists — bad, bad things," our teacher told us.

He was tired of our questions, and I was tired of being brave, so I never asked him what imperialist *meant. The word was all over the city, on banners and spray painted on walls: "Down with imperialists," in Persian and English. I secretly enjoyed watching the big bonfire of books in our school courtyard. I wasn't so into Shakespeare as a first-grader anyway.* Noddy *was more my thing, though* The Adventures of Noddy *was also written by an imperialist Brit — but translated into Persian, which means censored into Persian after the Revolution.*

I wonder if Agha Jerzy Grotowski's Towards a Poor Theater, *which I'm translating now, was ever burned here? There must have been a number of copies hanging around after the Revolution, because Grotowski was supposedly a major influence—he even came to the Shiraz Theater Festival.*

At a time when the regime was anything but poor or stark (it sported fur coronation gowns and crowns studded with rubies, diamonds, emeralds and sapphires that weighed more than the monarchs' own heads) Grotowski called for a stripping away of all embellishment, all pomp and frill—all that was unnecessary (costumes, sound effects, makeup, sets, lighting) until there stood only a naked, vulnerable actor.

We can't do naked, but we can do vulnerable—we can strip away the identity that's been forced on us.

Monday night, late . . .
Leili handed me a stack of photographs she took. They weren't at all what I had expected. I don't know why I thought she'd start on a more intimate level; she seems the type that would be a keen observer of detail, someone who might get in close to a weed growing from a crack in the sidewalk (plenty of those in this city, some of the only green we ever see). But instead she's given me large panoramas:

A ribbon of freeway leading east west, north and south like a bow tied on the top of a large gray box and covered in chaotic, colorful wrapping paper of little matchbox cars. She must have taken the photo standing on the overpass near Jordan. It's a perpetual traffic jam.

A mushrooming of little white plastic-roofed huts around a jungle of concrete high-rises.

The door to one of the white huts.

Rows of white buckets filled with long-stemmed flowers of every color, including blue carnations, lilies, baby's breath and jasmine.

A laborer with a threadbare shirt and baggy pants, plastic slippers and an old brown V-neck sweater taking money in exchange for a bouquet that he's just wrapped.

A dangle of lightbulbs across the top of a worker's tarp.

Newspapers laid out along the ground and sold alongside children's coloring books and the latest magazine editions of Today's Woman, Film, Soccer Fan, *and* The Mechanical Age.

A medical supply store along Revolution Street: skeletons, stethoscopes and scrubs.

I've looked at these ten times. They feel too Brazil, *too* Metropolis, *too cosmopolitan. Something's missing.*

Wednesday morning . . .

Tehran is an oozing amoeba that would have continued to sprawl had the Alborz mountain range not gotten in its way and forced it to either spill out into dry, remote areas outside of the mountain valley or on top of itself in a concrete forest of too-tall apartment buildings (problematic, as most aren't built to code and we are on a major earthquake fault). It's a hard place to escape and full of faults. It's a natural prison that we work hard at escaping: migrating, isolating ourselves at home, or running to the mountains and provinces. While the mountains suffocate Tehran in their tight clasp, they also provide an escape out and above. But our best escape is to go down: six feet down. The rich go up, the poor go under . . . sometimes in coffins. Makes me think of Shakespeare: "My words fly up, my thoughts remain below, words without thoughts never to heaven go."

Thursday at Naderi . . .

I figured it out! It took a while because I'm so good at ignoring it. I was walking to Naderi this morning and I looked up and who should be staring down at me but Martyr Avini, and I got it: Leili's managed to completely cut out all the propaganda! It must have been our conversation about Grotowski's theater and his all-black sets. We who live in a world that feels like it's been wrapped in layers of political banners need a theater of stark black nothingness. We've been mummified in propaganda—especially women with their chadors and rupushes.

Leili says we're like a generation of Shireen Neshat photos come to life. We've been written on and defaced by political and religious messages. You can't pass three blocks of any main street without seeing the mural of a religious figure, a martyr or a quote from the Quran or one of our many spiritual leaders' serious faces watching us. We have to turn away from our screaming city and all of its political noise and go inward. We'll change the stage or the frame or our minds. A psychic resistance entails a lot of meditation. Completely detached, we'll resist the lure of the undesirable world by creating another world inside our heads. We'll meditate and then walk away like sleepwalkers: somnambulists by day, alive by night.

Tea and Sympathy

The busses are backed up four or five rows deep, taxis are honking and not even the pedestrians are making much progress through the density of noise, smog, metal and flesh that is evening rush hour in Tehran.

Leili stops walking for a moment and takes the corner of her blue russari and holds it to her nose. The only people really moving along the street, despite the mirage of frenetic energy, are the motorcycles—delivering mail, food, people and in one instance, an entire family. The father drives the motorcycle, steering and pumping the pedals (preserving benzene), while his two young girls sit sidesaddle in front of him. His wife clutches his waist behind him for dear life, allowing only a small space for their bundled baby's head to bob back and forth out of the opening in her chador.

Leili's missed every meal Saqi cooked for her this week and has promised her that she'll be home for dinner. However, if she doesn't find a better mode of transportation than to stand in place dodging motorcycles on the sidewalk, she'll be lucky to make it home by the late prayers.

"Slow down!" Leili yells at the next motorcycle that nearly misses her. The driver, to her surprise, slows down.

"Great," Leili mutters and tries to move away.

"Get on," a female voice yells to her.

She turns, startled to see that under the driver's silver helmet is a woman's face covered with large shades.

"Leili," the driver says, taking off her glasses, "It's me."

"I didn't recognize you," Leili says, taking in Arezoo's new prairie dress that she wears as a rupush over black cargo pants. Arezoo's style has become less ingénue and more Bohemian art student. Her lips are painted blood red and her newly cut, trendy bangs peek out in a subtle zigzag below her colorful tribal scarf.

"I'm going to Tajrish. I can take you that far."

Leili pauses; she's never been on a scooter. "I didn't know you had a scooter . . ."

"Boyfriend's. Hop on, I'm late."

Leili awkwardly climbs on the back. Arezoo revs the engine and takes off on a sharp turn.

The scooter winds its way along the sidewalk, nearly missing schoolchildren, a man with a handcart delivering fruit, an old woman in a long, dirty black calico dress, her hand extended for alms, and a man pushing a cartload of uncovered women's mannequin legs into a lingerie boutique. The wind whips through with such force that Leili's hands shoot up to keep her russari from blowing off. She jerks backwards and feels a rush of adrenaline when she realizes that she isn't holding on—she clutches Arezoo's shoulder.

"You OK?" Arezoo shouts. As they zip and cut through the city, Leili revels in the rush of air, the absolute freedom. "Yes!" Leili shouts back.

Arezoo pulls up to a parked cab, idles the motor and nudges the kickstand with her heel.

"This is your stop," she says. Leili doesn't move.

Arezoo turns to Leili. "Need help?" she asks impatiently.

"No," Leili says. The bike may have stopped but Arezoo has clearly not slowed down, nor has the whirling in Leili's head.

She musters everything she can to swing her leg off the bike and stand up without vomiting. "Thanks," Leili stutters.

"No problem." Arezoo makes a quick appraisal of Leili's balance before zooming off.

Leili fills her mug from the pot warming on top of the samovar. She lodges a sugar cube in her cheek and sucks the hot tea through the melting sugar to sweeten the bitter bergamot.

The smell of freshly washed parsley fills the kitchen. A faint neon glow warms the table where Leili sets down her mug.

Saqi loves to cook and is already at the sink chopping vegetables as if she's preparing for a party—the more people, the better. When Leili was a young child, during the war, before everyone left, the house was abuzz with words and with the scent of saffron and steamed rice. Now it's only ever the three of them.

"Do you need help?" She asks her mother.

"No, thank you, but it's good to have your company." Saqi dries her hands and walks to the table. "I wasn't sure you'd make it in time; sit down."

"I've been working on a lab project. It's due soon."

"Sefat says you'll fall in love soon," Saqi giggles.

Leili's eyes widen for an instant. "Sefat is a nosey neighbor and an amateur fortune-teller; she says a lot of meaningless things," she says too quickly.

"And not to a Christian."

"Does that matter?" Leili asks, trying hard to keep her voice steady.

"Not to me. You were never very intesrested in church anyway. Such a rebellious child you were." Saqi studies Leili. "I let you down," she says, looking away.

"How?" Leili looks at her.

"Oh, being complicit. Forcing rituals that none of us believed in anymore," Saqi says. "Just to hold onto something that we had already lost well before the Revolution."

"Lost?"

"Our faith," Saqi says.

"You didn't have any faith?"

"Surprised? Not in God. My only faith was in you and your rebellious spirit. It was hard for us parents not to want our children to be defiant when we didn't believe in the things your teachers were teaching you."

"Yes, but church . . ."

"Religion is religion, and it all soured after the Revolution. Didn't matter what our faith, we felt God had turned his back on us."

"But you made me go . . . every week . . . ," Leili says.

"That was your father."

"But you sat there . . ."

"Yes, silently, but not insignificantly. I never told him about the novel you hid in your hymnal, or that you snuck out the back door of the church on your way to the bathroom halfway through mass," Saqi grins.

Leili puts her hand to her mouth and laughs.

"You knew?"

"I watched your shadow, like an angel, dance across the stained glass to freedom." Saqi sighs, and continues: "I wanted to be more like you. Once I followed you across the street to *Lord* for a café glacé. But then I saw you sitting there in the window, giggling with Shadi and I went back to church."

She looks at her mother, dumbfounded. Saqi reaches out and brushes Leili's cheek. "I'm sure your project will be wonderful," she says.

Leili frowns.

"What's bothering you?" Saqi prods gently.

Leili looks up at her mother. "I," she pauses, "Nothing." The lie seeps out despite her, like other lies she has spilled and lost along the way. "Drama," she mutters.

"Drama?" Saqi asks.

"I'm being dramatic."

"Just be careful," Saqi says, "But not too careful." She leans over and kisses the top of her daughter's head.

بسم الله الرحمن الرحيم

In the Name of God

Silence. Like corpses in war, they lie on the floor next to one another, staring up into the dark, damp and cold space. A candle is lit. It flickers and dances with the dark shadows across the walls.

Leili gave me a photograph of a man carrying a dead body down the trail in Darband. Another suicide. Another kind of martyrdom.

What do I really know about my main character? Why am I chasing and putting under the spotlight the most elusive persona in Iran? Everything is hearsay until I find the character's motivation. Nima tells me to be patient. That another topic will present itself. "You'll move on." He hopes. But I'm obsessed with the one thing I missed, with the part of the story that I didn't participate in—that made me less than everyone else. The war held whole neighborhoods together, however hostilely. My main character . . . whoever he or she is . . . is silent. But the other ghosts are not.

I just saw a bootlegged DVD called War Photographer: *The photographer in it asks his editor to darken the sky in his Balkans war photo. "It was darker that day," he says. The camera picked up the real color of the sky but the photographer's eye caught the tone, the feel of "the real." We are never a sum total of our recording instruments . . . be they pens, cameras or tape recorders. I'm going after a tone. Can they censor a tone if I leave out all the facts?*

Bodies are political: how they move, dress, when and where they appear. We either threaten or uphold the state's idea of a good Islamic citizen.

But then what of expression? If the body is covered then the face must speak.

Agha Jerzy cautions us, however, not to "build up a box of tricks." He worries that too much expression and too much emphasis on the surface will lead to a hollow inside. He says, "The force of gravity in our work pushes the actor towards an interior ripening which expresses itself through a willingness to break through barriers, to search for a . . . totality." I'll keep that in mind, but then how? What's left when we can't physically move in a provocative manner? What if we can't use anything but our faces? If we revealed how we truly feel, we wouldn't survive. We are nothing here without a box of tricks.

I met Leili for coffee again tonight. It's tough. I want to run after her, beg her to talk . . . watch her hands dance through the air as she explains her latest desires, worries, creations. Agha Jerzy would not approve. He says: "An act of creation . . . demands a maximum of silence and a minimum of words." Am I taking him too literally? He warns his actors that even outside of rehearsal the creative process is germinating and could be disturbed by "private ideas of fun," which he says, "have no place in the actor's calling." Agha Jerzy is becoming a bore, or worse, another guru, and if that's the case, then does theater become another religion? Another cult, with Grotowski as its charismatic leader? How to avoid this? Well, he's dead, for one, which helps, but then so is Khomeini. The dead can be more powerful than the living. Maybe it's not expecting, not wanting, not asking anything from the charismatic leader, or anyone else for that matter, that makes all the difference. The act of being completely independent?

The Swamp

They no longer need to pretend that they're walking through a swamp to slow down motion: the womb, what they call the theater basement, feels like a subterranean gutter. The heater of the entire theater complex is housed in the basement and it's been turned on for the season. It is hot and humid, and the air sets them heavily in space like figures suspended in Jell-O. Leili's long hair sticks to her head, face, and neck as she wiggles through the heat. She fantasizes about shaving her hair off like a girl who walked around Tehran like a boy.

Arezoo, who is always looking right at Hooman for direction, is now avoiding Hooman's gaze.

"Arezoo?" Hooman asks. She doesn't answer—he doesn't look away. "What happened to your eye?"

Leili looks more carefully and can just barely make out a shadow of green bruising around Arezoo's right eye.

"Nothing. Let it go."

"Someone's a little touchy," Kamran quips.

"I'm not touchy," Arezoo shoots back.

"Angry?" Nima suggests.

Arezoo looks up at him.

Leili moves away from her. Nima moves in closer.

"You scare people," Kamran says. "Does that make you feel powerful or just lonely?"

Arezoo lunges at him; he deftly steps away and she falls.

"I like that move. I'm writing it down," Hooman says writing. He looks up at Nima and asks, "We know that she is about to lunge, that she is angry and that her anger will propel her foreword, but does it? What does she do?" Hooman crouches down and looks up at Arezoo.

She looks confused.

"What does she do?" he repeats.

Hooman motions for Nima to come and stand behind him. Leili moves further around the circle until she can see them safely, from a distance. Kamran stops smirking and pays very close attention.

Hooman prods her: "You are angry, don't forget how angry you are. What are you going to do?"

Arezoo lurches forward a bit and then steps back.

"You're not ready to channel your anger just yet. Take a minute, breathe, and close your eyes. Don't rush this." Hooman waits a few minutes and then says, "What are you going to do?"

And then, in the silence, without moving, Arezoo lets out a bottomless, sorrowful, wounded scream.

Goose bumps prickle at Leili's skin. Her throat feels like it's closing. She listens closely for the warning sound of combat boots approaching their makeshift door. She instinctively moves toward the door and halfway up the stairs, where she is when Arezoo's voice falls to a lull. Leili is relieved to hear the sounds of horns and people; the city is louder and angrier then Arezoo.

"Excellent!" Hooman exclaims.

Arezoo clears her throat and grins.

"Grotowski says that two impulses arise and that the first should almost always be avoided. It is an empty reaction that only gets us in trouble."

"Not him again," Nima moans.

"What if we only have one reaction?" Kamran asks.

"Then you're a wolf acting on instinct. Humans have the

advantage of time. We can wait and sit with our emotions and discomfort until a second impulse comes—the creative instinct. That's the instinct we're after."

"What if it's just noise?" Kamran asks. He gives Arezoo a sharp look.

"Noise?" Nima asks.

"Noise?" Arezoo dares Kamran.

"The noise outside?" Leili suggests.

"How are we going to practice safely with Arezoo screaming her bloody head off?" Kamran asks.

"Arezoo's voice is a muscle, a separate actor," Hooman is curt.

Kamran laughs.

"You have connections in the studio world," Hooman says to Kamran. "I'm sure you can find some sort of sound studio where Arezoo can work on vocals?"

"Where she can safely scream her bloody head off in a sound-proof cave? Sure," Kamran says.

Arezoo gives Hooman a grateful smile.

"Candle's almost out." Leili points to the dying candle.

Nima goes to their makeshift prop box and returns empty-handed.

"I just bought a new box on Monday," Leili says.

"We must have used them," Arezoo insists.

"In two days? Impossible."

"Where did you put them?"

"In the prop box."

"Lie down for your final stretches," Hooman commands. He walks around them, gently, bending down to cradle a head in his hands, pulling and stretching a neck, pushing down on a set of shoulders, especially Leili's, which always spring back up and cave in to protect her chest. "Grow longer," he whispers to her.

"I'm taking too much space; what about the others?" Leili asks.

"This is your chance to be more assertive, to stop thinking about your space on earth in relation to everyone else. Be a little *poru*, go for it."

Leili wiggles over a little, and then stops.

"Making yourself small is a hard habit to break," Hooman says.

Leili looks behind her.

"Look inside," Hooman whispers. "You're dowsers passing over unexplored territory," Hooman encourages.

Leili closes her eyes.

"Theater reveals the darkness within. Theater, like the dark, is a provocation," Hooman whispers. Kamran chuckles.

"How do you feel?" Hooman asks, stretching Nima's legs away from him.

"Tight," says Nima.

"Grounded, safe," answers Leili.

"Dirty," says Arezoo, wiping her sweaty forehead for emphasis.

They get up and move about quietly, donning winter coats and packing up bags.

Leili waits outside for Hooman, who darts past her with a quick "good-bye." He walks rapidly to the traffic circle. She follows him. "Hooman," she calls after him. He turns quickly, caught off guard, carefully sheltering the cigarette he tries to light.

"Thank you," she whispers into the cool air as she turns and walks the other way.

"See you tomorrow," he calls to her back.

"See you," she says, but lingers a minute longer. She's not ready to go home—she wishes practices were longer. She crosses the street and looks back one last time at Hooman, who walks toward the bookstores. As she's about to turn, she sees Arezoo catch up to him. Leili watches her walk alongside him until they're lost in the crowds.

بسم الله الرحمن الرحيم

In the Name of God

When I'm a little lost I read theory for inspiration—in stanzas and snippets, the way I would poetry, like this idea from Hannah Arendt's introduction to Benjamin's Illuminations *that language "enables us to give material form to the invisible." Page 14, if you ever find a copy. Pure poetry, you get my point? Am I giving material form to the invisible or making it more opaque?*

I spend my nights underground translating dead authors like a badger gnawing its way out of its own den until a beam of sunlight through the stairwell tells me it is safe to leave. Is it worth it? Does anyone ever actually use the theory in these banned books?

These books give me the illusion that I'm connected to some larger community somewhere in the world. But then I try to think of examples of other people putting these writings into practice and I start feeling depressed, scared and more isolated than ever because I can't think of a single example. Does everyone else in the world have so much economic, political and creative freedom that they don't have to turn to theory? Doubt it. It's as though that imagined community of like minds has disappeared—over time devoured slowly by one snake and then another.

Bazaar

Tajrish bazaar's miniature mouth is tucked away behind the bus depot and rows of resting pink and yellow city buses that look like freshly colored Easter eggs. The narrow opening makes it feel that much more exclusive once inside. Leili walks through a nest of fruit sellers, pears, plums and bananas piled high on cardboard boxes and folding tables underneath a rope of electricity from which a single lightbulb dangles dangerously close to the pineapples.

She buys cardamom, cumin and clove in permeable plastic bags to place in her room in order to drown out the smell of her father's cigarettes.

The bazaar is just waking from its afternoon siesta, still sleepy and quiet, calm and peaceful and full of space to wander aimlessly examining cutlery and cookware, Turkoman wool socks, blue-glazed *galiyoons*, Hookah pipes, birdseed and sweets. The sleepy rhythm of the bazaar invites her to stop and look without being pushed and shoved aside or moved along rapidly like a twig in the rush of an angry river. She prefers Tehran's calm undercurrent to its torrid and rapid surface.

Leili ambles along from storefront to storefront, where shopkeepers sit in chairs outside their doors, sipping tea and offering buckets of goods to shoppers too hurried to stop inside.

Leili is rummaging through a bucket of bright yellow plastic slippers when she hears someone call her name. She turns to find Nima walking rapidly toward her.

"Shopping?" he asks.

"Sort of."

"They're fake," Nima says.

"Obviously, Adidas is spelled Adidos," Leili laughs. "But they're really soft and my feet are always sore after practice."

"Mine, too," Nima says.

"You shopping?"

"Visiting . . . my dad," Nima says.

"Oh." Leili looks around.

"He's a shopkeeper."

"Really?"

"And no . . . , I don't plan on running the family business any-time soon."

"Sorry. You must get surprised looks a lot."

"It's OK, I'm used to it. I'm not a typical *bazaari* boy. No hair gel or tight Puma shirts. That's the nouveau merchant class. Want to meet him?"

"Depends—does he wear tight Puma shirts?" Leili jokes.

"No. Baggy suits—old-school bazaar. The family's been here for generations. My mother, on the other hand . . ."

Nima takes Leili to the far end of the bazaar where the old nineteenth-century Qajar Entrance was demolished and the bazaar extended into a small two-story mall.

Nima's father is shorter than Nima, but has the same curly hair and bright smile. He ushers Leili in and presses her with tea and biscuits.

"We just got a shipment of MP3 players . . . newest thing on the market," he says, pulling a few out of a large box marked "Beijing Transport." He unwraps a sleek silver one and hands it to Leili. She turns it in her hand and admires its compact size and sheen.

"Nima is doing all the engineering."

"I'd hardly call it that."

"What are you doing?" she asks, handing the player back to Nima's father.

"Keep it," he says.

"I couldn't," Leili demures.

"Please, any friend of Nima's is worth gold—this is nothing, it's silver." He winks.

Leili thanks him and takes the player.

"So how do you program this?" she asks Nima. "Is that what you do, program them?"

Nima looks away from her out at the alley where a swarm of police and Komiteh rush by.

"Hardly. I load them with music." He finally says, "They're useless without music. I break through the government firewall and download music. It's my little contribution to society. What do you like?"

"Music?"

Nima takes the player from her. "I'll surprise you," he promises, walking away.

"So . . . you're at university," Nima's father starts to ask, when the bell on the front door jingles and a policeman walks in.

"Seen any young men run by?"

"No," he shakes his head. "Tea?"

"Not now, Sayyed Agha, thank you, another time."

When the men leave, he turns back to Leili and asks, "Do you know Arezoo?" His eyes twinkle when he says her name.

"Yes," Leili answers.

"Lovely girl. One day . . ."

"Dad!" Nima admonishes his father from the back room.

"She's a lot like his mother. I married my opposite, the daughter of my father's competitor. Nouveau Bazzari. Nima is like me . . . he's a simple boy, content. He doesn't have any artistic or material aspirations."

"Really?" Leili says loud enough for Nima to hear.

"Not really, I just happened upon friends that do," Nima answers.

"Hooman?"

"We were randomly assigned roommates," Nima says.

"He wants a family. He enjoys what he does."

"Dad, enough."

His father leans toward Leili and whispers, "He finds what he needs in this city. Not his mother. She's always redecorating and bemoaning the fact that she doesn't live in L.A. But she's spunky and lively and kind. Arezoo has that same kindness."

"You've met her?" Leili tries to sound polite.

"Briefly."

"Allah-o-Akbar . . ." The call to prayer begins. Nima's father rises. "With your permission," he says. "We have another room and a spare kit, if you'd like to pray."

"Thank you, not now," Leili says.

"In that case, stay. Nima and I won't be long."

Nima returns with her player. "Stay for dinner?"

"I can't . . . ," Leili stammers. "Thank you." She smiles at Nima, who locks the door after her and goes to join his father for the prayers.

بسم الله الرحمن الرحيم
In the Name of God

They say that a director is key. I need a mentor. There's a guy who broke all the rules during Khatami's presidency but no one knows where he is. I met some of his actors at Naderi. They claim they've lost touch. Did something happen? They looked at each other oddly when I asked. Hard-wired loyalty. Is he still alive? Did he leave the country? Is he in prison? A journalist would have asked, but I didn't want to pry. He taught them well—not even an uncomfortable shift in the chair, clearing of the throat, subtle change of subject, nothing betrayed.

November 8, 2008
Arezoo took a theater class where they walked like ants the entire term. They were meant to be a colony of ants . . . crawling around the cold stone floor. She said her teacher wore white canvas givehs. *She remembers his shoes but not his name.*

Did you ever look into his face? I asked. Would you recognize him now? She hasn't a clue.

She said she respected him, yes, but was careful not to care too much. Why? I asked.

She said a friend once told her that immature actors look for gurus. A mature actor knows that you cannot mimic a real master but instead must meet his/her challenges.

It's so much bigger than that. We're not looking for gurus—our country has had enough of those. And yet the New Age stuff, which may look different, is dangerously similar, and perilously popular.

The play . . . How do I even begin to write a play? I need an inciting moment, then an obstacle followed by a few personal blocks—that pretty much describes daily life. What's so new and exciting about that? I want to educate, to change and open minds.

Use an ancient legend, Nima suggests. All of our ancient legends are about battle. How boring. But then, they're so relevant still. I could write a modern Rostam and Sohrab story, another Shahnameh. Rostam, a warrior, the strongest hero in the land, has an affair with a beautiful princess in a foreign city. He leaves her bed in the night never to return. He does, however, gift her a valuable bracelet that identifies her bond with him. Nine months later she gives birth to a strong, handsome boy, Sohrab. Everyone in the town can tell that there is something special about the boy, but the woman, Roodabeh, never reveals his lineage. One day the young hero Sohrab goes on a military mission. His mother begs him not to go. Before he leaves she puts the bracelet on his arm.

The battle is fierce and comes down to two heroes on either side, Rostam and Sohrab. Rostam recognizes the bracelet and his son only after he has mortally wounded him.

All Night

"Practice is over. I have music. It's American, from an all-Black modern dance company. Don't be put off by the fact that it's a little religious . . . the stories are based on the Bible but remember, they're just stories. They're called spirituals. We don't have any visuals of the group performing; we can try to visualize how they may have interpreted this music, but it's more important how we interpret it, how it moves us."

"What about butoh?" asks Arezoo.

"The really slow Japanese dance?" asks Nima.

"Personally, I'd rather play a woman in a Kabuki show," says Kamran. They ignore him.

"Bring in all of your ideas. Listen up . . . They've stopped heating the building. It's too cold to continue down here."

Leili's heart beats fast. She looks at her shoes—she doesn't want to hear what he's about to announce.

"We're going to break for a month. Please do the stretching exercises. We'll still have enough time to rehearse for the student theater fest this spring if we resume before Nowruz."

There are a few grunts and nods of resignation.

Leili looks at Hooman. "It's just a break," he says.

Outside, Hooman catches Leili on the corner before she crosses the street. "Leili," he calls in his above-ground voice. It lacks the depth of their kept silences and surprises her. It's been weeks since they've spoken above ground.

She turns toward him. "Yes?"

"Ever been to the all-night café?"

"No," Leili grins.

"Are you expected at home?"

She shakes her head, no.

"Let's go," Hooman says, directing her toward the fountain exit, where they find Arezoo approaching the park.

"Practice already over? Where to?" she asks casually.

"Where have you been all week?" Hooman sounds angry.

She looks around nervously. "Here . . . I mean, around."

"Here?" Leili asks.

"Which way are you headed? I'll walk with you." Arezoo cuts Leili off to get closer to Hooman.

Hooman points ahead to Revolution Street and starts to walk. He turns to Arezoo. "So?"

"I'm tired. I've been resting," she replies curtly. "Where are you headed to, anyway?"

Hooman softens his tone: "The all-night café."

"Fun, I'll join you," she says. She gives Leili a controlled smile. "Just a minute, I need to run to the bathroom."

"In the park?" Leili asks. "It's dirty, dangerous."

"I'm a big girl. I'll meet you there." Arezoo turns back toward the park without waiting for a reply.

"Leave her," Hooman says. He takes Leili through a maze of little alleys behind the theater.

"How do they get cars down these streets?" asks Leili.

"They don't. These streets were built when Tehran was a village back in the donkey years."

"Even that building?" Leili points to a beautiful brick building surrounded by an old brick wall.

"It was a summer palace, and then the home of the famous

French philosopher Henri Corbin and now it's the philosophy institute. I buy books there sometimes."

Their walk ends in a small festive square where, despite the cold and the late hour, groups of friends, mostly students and young office professionals, gather on the sidewalk, holding thin plastic cups of hot coffee and cocoa. They shift their drinks back and forth from one cold or hot hand to the other. Those still waiting for drinks hop from one foot to the other to stay warm.

"Wow, where did all these people come from and how did they know about this place?" Leili asks. "It's like Luna Park at midnight, only for well-dressed adults!"

"Funny, huh? First time I came here was seven years ago, before all the other boutique restaurants joined in. The café was a lone beacon of light amid a crowd of revelers. It was more *khaki*, down-to-earth, back then and more dangerous to be out at night. The scene reminded me of a film about the Balkans, where during the war people came above ground in the fog . . . when it was safe. Imagine crawling out into the fog and discovering other people in the mist, so candidly, so enjoyably."

"It kind of feels like we're in a movie or a painting. Ever seen the American painting of a café late at night?"

"Edward Hopper?" Hooman asks.

"Yes! The dark blue window casing against the snow makes the coffee shop look like that painting."

"Maybe you should paint it," Arezoo suggests as she comes up behind them. Leili shoots Hooman a questioning look.

"That was fast," Hooman says, ignoring Arezoo's sarcasm and Leili's piercing look.

"I'll order," Leili offers.

"Go for it," says Arezoo.

Leili crowds her way into the tiny coffee bar where muted exhales fog the window. The warm interior light is focused, like that of a museum display, on shelves filled with colorfully wrapped foreign sweets, jars of Nutella, Nescafé and Cadbury cocoa tins. Before she's figured out where the line begins and ends, the barista barks at her over a blender of frothed milk and bananas: "Order?"

"Me?" Leili asks.

"What do you want?"

"Espresso, cappuccino and hot chocolate."

"Wait outside. It's too crowded in here."

Leili scurries back to Hooman and Arezoo. "Did you see the foreigner in there?" She points to the coffee shop window. They all three squint at the steamy window.

"It's odd, a foreigner in this part of town," says Leili. "I didn't even know about this place."

"Well, you wouldn't," Arezoo says. Hooman eyes her. "What?" Arezoo purrs. "Westerners always know more than the locals. My friend's family went to Istanbul when her uncle worked for Iran Air. When they got lost the locals only confused them, so they got in the habit of finding a German with a guidebook."

"We're really far south. Doesn't this street lead to the bazaar?" Leili asks.

Hooman nods his head. "You really don't get out much," he says, amused.

"Maybe she was at the Golestan Palace Museum and headed out in the wrong direction," Arezoo says absently, distracted.

"Who?" Hooman asks.

"The foreigner."

"The museum closed hours ago. She has to be a tourist; no Iranian woman would dare go out alone to an all-night café," Leili comments. Arezoo raises her eyebrows.

"Tourist?" Hooman laughs. "Iran doesn't have tourists. Why would anyone come here? We still have bullet holes in the parliament building from the constitutional Revolution."

"I went to see the Archeology Museum last week," Leili says.

"Really?"

"And were there masses of people there?" Arezoo asks.

Hooman shoots Arezoo a critical look. "A tad edgy tonight," he comments.

Leili ignores their exchange and says, "Actually, I was the only one at the museum. The guard ran ahead of me to each case and turned on the light as I approached. It only cost two rials!"

"You're kidding," Hooman says.

"Ticket prices haven't changed since 1979," Leili tells him.

"That's a lot of inflation in thirty years!"

"And yet silly folks pay hundreds a month for cell phone lines when Pahlavi-era public phones still take a single rial coin."

"Yes, but finding and buying those coins is like investing in an antique chair," Arezoo comments.

Hooman laughs. Leili turns her attention back to the foreigner.

"It must take a lot of confidence to come here alone," Leili says softly.

"You could; you went to the museum," Hooman says.

Arezoo rolls her eyes. "Why aren't you doing the exercises with us?" she asks Hooman pointedly. She inches toward him so as to cut Leili out of their circle. Hooman looks up at her thoughtfully.

"Sorry, did the question surprise you?" Arezoo asks bluntly.

"Maybe a little. Isn't a director always on the outside, watching? It's best in the theater not to get too close to your actors. Or so I read anyway," he says softly; he bites his lip and looks at Leili.

"You're close to Nima," Arezoo challenges.

"Nima's doing this as a favor," Hooman reminds her.

"He's a good friend to spend so much time on a project that has nothing to do with his career," Leili says.

"Theater is more than just a career," Arezoo snaps.

Leili's cheeks burn.

"I didn't mean to imply that acting isn't important. I just meant that he is dedicated—a friend that would do anything for you."

"I would do anything for you," Hooman says. He squeezes her arm. She blushes.

"I'll go get our coffees," Arezoo says, and briskly walks away. Leili looks around. "What's with her?" she asks Hooman.

"Maybe she's unearthed something. The exercises can have that effect. They can unearth pain stored deep in the actor's muscles."

"Muscles hold pain?" Leili asks.

"And memory," Hooman says. Leili bites her fingernails. Hooman gently takes her hand.

"Bad habit," she admits, burying her hands in her pocket.

"Nervous?"

"It's a cool crowd—where are the Komiteh? They'd make a killing on bribes," she says. She looks around wishing she smoked or had something to fidget with.

"They make an even bigger profit from the store owners," Hooman responds. "I've seen them."

"Unless the store owners have the right family members," Leili suggests.

"What do you mean?" Hooman asks absently. He watches the foreign woman give something to Arezoo. It's too blurry to see through the window, but it looked like a piece of paper: an address, a note or money?

"You know, dead ones: a martyr, a POW, who knows?"

Hooman looks at her pointedly, "It's not at all like that for those families," he says.

"Sorry." Leili quickly changes the subject. "Thank you."

"For what?"

"For including me. You know I don't act and . . . I'm a bit of a risk."

"No more than any of us are."

"I love rehearsals, even if I'm not so good."

"Why say you're not good?"

"It's easy for you. You're exceptional, top of your class— gifted," she says. Hooman laughs.

"I bought the notion that if I could be an engineering major then I could do anything." Leili blushes deeply.

"Such as?"

"Art."

"Art isn't about intelligence; it's about imagination—more valuable and sorely underrated." Hooman nudges her playfully.

"I know . . . ," she says, discouraged.

"Do you really? Don't claim defeat so quickly," Hooman suggests.

"Right. No point, really. I haven't a clue what it is that I lack as a painter. It's unfair to give someone passion without talent. It's not just talent I lack. It's that I don't see things the way I'm supposed to. Does that make sense?"

"No. Why would you want to see things like everyone else? Haven't we had enough conformity?"

"I mean as an artist. I can't paint. I have this vision that I just can't get out."

"Painting isn't the only way to create a vision. What about your photography?"

Leili frowns. "It's just that, well . . ."

"You're not used to struggling, are you?"

Her cheeks burn.

"Didn't think so." Hooman lights a cigarette.

"Struggle is good practice for humility. And humility is a vital part of art . . . that's why rug weavers always leave a single imperfection—only God can create perfection. Like this snowflake," he says. He brushes a small dusting of snow off her russari.

"Coffee's here," Arezoo announces. She approaches with a wobbly plastic tray. Leili retrieves what's left of her hot chocolate and leaves the rest dripping off the sides of the tray. She looks beyond Arezoo at the foreigner, who is dressed in black Doc Martens boots, jeans, a wool peacoat and a brown wool russari that accentuates her round face and green eyes. The woman swirls her straw around the sides of her drink as if she were holding a cocktail.

"She dresses like you," Leili teases Hooman. He laughs.

"I forgot napkins," Arezoo says. She walks briskly back toward the café. They both watch Arezoo approach the foreigner.

When Arezoo returns, Leili asks, "Do you know her? Invite her over."

"There's enough policing here without you nosing into people's business," Arezoo snaps.

Leili turns sharply. Her scarf slips and reveals a shaft of straight shiny chestnut-colored hair. "I'm going for a walk," she calls back. Snowflakes melt into inky puddles on her exposed hair the minute they land. She pulls her russari back over her head and ties it more tightly around her face.

As Leili disappears toward the main square, she can barely hear Hooman say, "Arezoo? What's with you?"

"I love snow," Hooman pants, trying to sound matter-of-fact as he catches up to Leili. He slips his reddening hands into his pockets. Leili turns to face him. She's wearing black stretch pants under a knee-length black hooded wool coat and knee-high black boots. Snowflakes gather on her eyelashes. Little specks of orange in her eyes—like a bronze patina—sparkle.

"Careful, that snowflake is causing your eyes to rust." Hooman's eyes meet hers.

"That's their natural color." Leili half-smiles as she asks, "Why is Arezoo so angry lately? She was always . . . determined. But, this is, I don't know, she's so . . ."

"I agree, it's not like her." Hooman looks down at the snow and says, "Boyfriend troubles, maybe?"

"Boyfriend? Does Nima know?"

"Yeah."

"She seems angry at you in particular," Leili says. "She was so energetic and enthused when we started and now she's skipping rehearsals."

"That's because I promised to let her sing."

"Arezoo sings?"

"She's in an underground rock band . . . I always forget the name . . . they put on concerts in garages and abandoned buildings and sometimes in people's homes. I'll take you sometime."

"A rock band?" Leili asks.

"Arezoo's boyfriend is the lead singer and she does back-up vocals—which she isn't thrilled about."

"Yeah, she's not really a back-up type."

"He lets her sing every now and then. But mostly he's paranoid that the government will find out. They don't have clearance from Ershad. He won't let her record, and she's paranoid that he recorded her and sold the CD in LA. He was there last summer and came back a celebrity."

"Paranoid with good reason. Why doesn't she dump him?"

"They sing together. It's a serious bond—art." He looks at her meaningfully. "Arezoo can be intimidating, but mean she isn't. She's tired and stressed. Forgive her." Hooman pauses, "You're young and in school and pretty and nice . . . it's intimidating for her," Hooman brushes her hand with his.

"Arezoo intimidated? Now you're teasing me." She shivers.

He comes closer and gently wipes her wet face. She blinks up at him just as he bends in to kiss her. She kisses him back and then quickly steps away.

"What if someone . . ." She looks around nervously. The formally political city, full of graffiti and murals, is now covered by a rupush of fresh white snow.

"It's as if we entered a different dimension," Leili says, looking around in wonder.

"Which way shall we walk? It's too cold to stand still," Hooman says, rubbing his hands together. The cuffs of his peacoat barely cover his long thin wrists.

They stroll side by side, crushing the white snow with their matching stride.

Hooman's breath is heavy and gray against the dense air. "It's too early for snow," he concludes.

"It figures that global warming in the rest of the world would be global cooling in Iran," Leili says. "When we were kids we had to wait until February for a good ski. My father loved the snow. On the first snowfall of every year, my parents stole me away from school to Park Mellat. We'd go to the center of the park, far from any prying Komiteh, drop ourselves down onto the soft cold clean snow and flutter like angels."

"Sounds nice."

"Yeah." Leili frowns.

"Wasn't it?" Hooman asks.

"It was, until one day I was fluttering around like a little angel and a Basij showed up out of nowhere." Leili stops.

"Did he hurt you?" Hooman asks.

"No. Worse. He made my dad shame me. He told him to retrieve his tramp." Leili kicks the snow with the tip of her boot. "My dad grabbed my arms and jerked me up off the snow like a common criminal." She looks down at the snow, sighs and then looks back up at Hooman.

"Forget them, it's not a crime to lie in the snow," Hooman says. "No one's around," he says and gently tugs at her arm.

Leili's face burns. "No!"

"Come on. Together on the count of three: one . . ." Hooman pulls her down with him. She squeals with delight despite herself but quickly stands.

Hooman flutters until he has made a large, bold angel. He stands, brushes off the snow and says, "You can't blame them anymore. Now you're just censoring yourself."

Leili's teeth chatter. "I want to stay here and watch the snowfall all night."

"If it were warmer, sure." He rubs his cold hands, "We should leave while there's still traction," he says, and grabs her hand. They trudge through the thickening snow back toward the café.

"I've never been up all night. You?" Leili says.

"Ask me when I last slept," Hooman laughs.

Leili says, thinking out loud, "You could have a parallel existence with all that extra time—especially if you know about places like this."

"I've been up writing a play," he says.

"Will we perform it?"

"Maybe."

"What's it about?"

"I'm not really sure yet."

Hooman takes a pouch of tobacco and a small thin piece of paper from his pocket and rolls a cigarette.

"Is that a Hafez fortune?" Leili comes closer to get a better look.

"Yeah, I'm out of cigarette paper."

"Maybe you shouldn't smoke."

"What?" Hooman laughs.

"You can't use that," Leili insists.

He stops rolling and asks, "Why not? These scraps collect in my pocket like lint." He gives her a curious smile. "I'm recycling."

"It's sacrilegious," she blurts out.

He smiles at her. "Are you worried about my future?" He finishes rolling his cigarette. Leili blushes and looks away.

Hooman lights his cigarette and Leili puts her hands on her hips and persists, "The ink is harmful. It's full of toxins."

He takes a purposefully long drag. "Don't worry. The tobacco will kill me faster than this ink." Hooman laughs and coughs. "Seriously, this fortune should burn," he says.

"What did it say?" she asks.

"I can't tell you. You know if someone looks at another's fortune it may come true."

She smiles—he believes in these things.

A taxi rounds the corner. Hooman drops his cigarette to wave the car down.

"Here," Leili says and hands him a strip of dusty paper with a number.

He turns the paper over and reads that Hafez has told her that she will find her soul mate.

"I'm glad you looked at it," she smiles. "Call me."

بسم الله الرحمن الرحيم

In the Name of God

Possession: a state where a person is alienated from her normal self and is spoken through by another.

How about a play within the play? Playing with information . . . playing. Playing is risky. Writing is risky. Does the motivation of the character always need to be clear? In Iran motivation is never clear. What other culture has ta'arrof—a social and therefore accepted lie.

End each act with a hook. I can't end with a hook, that's ridiculous.

Leili's scared of heights. It's endearing. She's trying to overcome all of her fears at once. I remember my fear. Not of heights, but of the depths I can go to when I'm not writing, moving one letter after the other in a neat little line of black and white.

But I understand her fears. Yoga was scary. My joints hold other kinds of pain, other physical memories of cold and damp nights when I was laid down to sleep in what had been a cramped grave for so many. Cold, wet earth seeped into my muscles, crawled into the tiny spaces and spread itself to stay. On those re-enactment trips to the former war front with my mother we had no science, no map to tell us what we'd find or feel when a tiny twist or a subtle turn unearthed a hidden well. But I stretched past the pain, past my buried rheumatic history, past the guilt of survival; it was my spirit that I was dowsing for in an early grave.

Every stretch released some forgotten wound. But the key is that it got released. It hurts and pinches a bit as the pain leaves but then it's gone—if you don't hold onto it. If you stop to judge it or linger in it or do anything more than observe it pass, it will stay and grow stronger. That's what I told Leili, anyway. She said she'd like to keep it buried where it is. Open up and let it out or it will kill you, I told her. She's holding her parents' pain. We all are. I think the play has to be about breaking free from the previous generation. Our parents protested, they created a revolution and look what it got them.

What will it take for us to move past our parents' history? Iran's mythology, the way we operate, is all about respecting an older generation that has done nothing worthy of our respect. Even if in most stories they're killing us or eating our brains out we're still told to respect our elders. When will the elders respect us? Take the theater, for example: because of the years of propaganda in our public education, our generation is good at writing plays that are acceptable to the government. And our theater elders hate us for it. They call us apologists and make it difficult for those of us who really are trying to subvert the system to succeed. Their refusal to allow us to work keeps all of us stuck in the dark ages as they suck the brains of the youth like snakes, killing their own sons like Rostam.

Pop Art

Leili inserts the earbuds of her new MP3 player and threads the wires underneath her rupush and slips the player into her pocket. She hastily throws her russari on and ties it in a knot at her chin. She checks herself in the mirror to make sure that no part of the player is visible and carefully reaches into her pocket, pokes her finger through the hole and presses Play.

The acrid air stings her dry throat and lips. Rush hour is in full swing, with honking horns and huffing busses moving people up and down the city and drowning out her music. She slips her hand into her pocket and raises the volume with her forefinger and thumb until the sound of flowing gutters and traffic fade back into Prince's urgent beat: "Life it ain't real funky / Unless it's got that pop . . ."

She walks to the traffic square, where the city sweeps her up and takes her into the crush of its anonymity. She passes an elementary school where unseen girls behind the wall and boys in front do their morning exercises. She subtly brushes her headscarf with her fingers and gingerly removes her right earpiece to hear the familiar chant: "One Allah," the children chant." "Sidebend," demands the megaphone. "Two Allah," "Reach over your head . . ." She misses those days when she was a child and didn't have to think about her future beyond recess.

She walks the city with the intensity of purpose and aimlessness of writing a journal, each step an exclamation point, each block a sentence.

Leili slips past the college gatekeeper—an easy feat, as the old man who sits on a milk crate, sipping tea and warming his hands over a kerosene heater, is half-blind and too busy tuning his radio to notice an intruder. "It is ten o'clock in the morning. This is Tehran. Today over a thousand remains of Iranian soldiers missing in Iraq will be returned to Iran . . ." Leili pauses to listen to the news before she pushes past the requisite post-Revolution privacy curtain and into the Bauhaus-style courtyard of the Faculty of Fine Art, where Arezoo is already waiting.

"You're late," she says.

"Sorry, busses were full."

"Just follow me in as if you belong in there and set up. The teacher is against attendance on principle."

"Are you sure?" Leili bites her lower lip.

"No risk, no gain," Arezoo says, turning on her heel.

The art studio is warmly lit by the strong morning sun and is already abuzz with chatter and laughter. Arezoo helps Leili find an available easel and hands her a charcoal vine.

Leili stands expectantly, steadying the easel with one hand, charcoal vine raised in the other, and her full attention on Arezoo.

"Don't look at me for direction. I've never drawn a thing in my life."

"Aren't you in this class?" Leili asks.

"No," Arezoo answers, "I told Hooman I'd help you."

"But . . ."

"Here's your man," Arezoo says.

A young, clean-shaven man dressed in dark jeans, a broad black leather belt with a silver cowboy buckle and an old gray V-neck sweater walks in and winks at Arezoo.

"Find a subject," he says without introduction. "Replicate its image. Be creative and draw what you see—that doesn't necessarily mean to draw what's there. We'll discuss the difference later. Right now, we are interested in lines, so find something with form—a good shape." He looks over at Arezoo meaningfully. "I have some eggs in this basket here if you need a model." The class laughs.

"Welcome to figurative art in the Islamic Republic," Arezoo whispers.

Leili finally gives up on drawing free-form and takes an egg from the front of the classroom. She is so engrossed in shading the egg that she doesn't notice that the instructor has announced a break.

"Put the charcoal down. Perfectionism kills creativity." He turns the easel she wipes and shoos her out of the room.

"Let's go get a juice," Arezoo suggests.

Arezoo orders drinks while Leili ponders the pomegranates on the counter: a would-be perfect circle disturbed by unorganized little bumps and indentations crowned with a bit of brown wiry brush that sprouts into a tiny spout at the top. Not an easy color: yellow, brown, pink and red.

"How do you know the instructor?" Leili asks, taking her juice from Arezoo.

"I modeled for him," Arezoo says. And then for emphasis adds, "With my clothes off."

Leili turns the color of her pomegranate juice. Arezoo laughs. "He's skilled—you'll learn a lot." Arezoo downs her orange juice and says, "I have to take off."

"Thank you," Leili says.

"Thank Hooman. I owed him a favor."

Leili turns back to the pomegranate and wonders: could she paint its moonlike surface if she didn't know the intricacies of its interior—a casing like an egg carton that holds edible rubies? Pomegranates, she decides, are not an amateur's fruit.

بسم الله الرحمن الرحيم

In the Name of God

I went to tie a ribbon, to make a wish at the shrine. I'd never noticed the hallway before. The black-and-white photos caught my eye and so I followed their trail of history from the Revolution to the War: Khomeini walking down the stairs of his return Air France flight, martyrs going off to war and then hands, millions of hands grasping at Khomeini's dead body as his casket was airlifted to Behesht-e Zahra cemetery. The pictures were a crumb trail that I followed all the way up to the second floor of the shrine and into a large salon covered with posters of wounded soldiers, army tanks, paintings of Khomeini and angelic mothers cradling their dead boys in their arms. In the corners of the salon muted television monitors played looped reels of frontline war footage. A tape recorder was set to the wrong speed: the music warbled, morbid and chilling. I should have left. But I didn't. All it took was a moment of hesitation and I walked further in to confront the ghosts.

I started out slowly, until I was almost running through the labyrinth of glass cases, peering down quickly into exhibits of everyday objects unearthed from the front. This was a makeshift martyr's museum. Old rusty razors and used toothbrushes rested in velvet like precious jewels. What ancient ritual did these everyday objects serve? Cleaning teeth for the afterlife? What kind of ritual must everyday life become when death waits so near? I shudder as I write. What can it mean for a society when a bar of soap, dirty socks, old sneakers, a melted metal fork and shards of a grenade are elevated to museum objects? I tried to convince myself that I am not a part of, but apart . . . an anthropologist, an archeologist examining without emotion.

Some display cases held birth and death certificates—mere bookends binding years that barely count past a decade. Uniform journals, almost none of them filled in, began with the same preprinted line: "Dear Family, Today my desire is to die the death of a martyr."

My ruse as anthropologist was over when I saw the case of personal snapshots taken by soldiers. They were grainy and printed on the same rough-textured Kodak paper, burned in the same corners, faded into the same muted browns and greens as my childhood pictures. Some of these boys may have known my dad, or been friends with my brother. My childhood pictures and these of the soldiers at the front may have been developed in the very same shop, mixed with the same chemicals that fixed my personal history into this bloody visual landscape. They could be hikers, these soldiers; there was no evidence save uniforms to the contrary—same landscape, same sun. But then, lying about carelessly at the bottom of the frame are guns.

I had an urgent desire to outrun the ghosts that would either chase me away or follow me to safety. I ran.

At the exit a banner claimed victory for all the martyrs of the Sacred Defense. If I were braver I'd come back in the middle of the night with spray paint and write: "No one can claim victory in a war where a single person has died."

Out in the street I squinted into the bright light, relieved. I walked slowly down the hill to a traffic circle. The hollow tap of the one-legged ghost faded, unable to compete with the din of Tehran. The silent haunting of a ghost is hardly competition for the deafening presence of life.

I sat on a street curb, head in hands, unable to shake the feeling that something has changed. I'm a cowardly collector of stories. Maybe I should slow down and stop trying to outrun the ghosts but let them lead me instead. Who knows where I could end up.

Tuesday the tenth . . .
Sifting through the debris, I have discovered the bones of my character's
vulnerability splintered by the risks that he took (those are recorded fact,
agreed upon by all). The skeleton, however shaky, is emerging.

Hu by the Fire

From Tajrish the streets wind upward through the mountains, deep into Niavaran, where the air is lighter, damper, and the houses and apartments don't lean into each other the way they do downtown, spilling over garbage and bad air. Here the houses are large pre-Revolution villas that have the dignity of privacy and space.

"I'm glad you called. It's strange not seeing you guys every week. A month feels like the longest winter," Leili says.

"It's already March," Hooman answers.

Leili changes the subject: "I love these old mud walls."

Hooman takes a long, deep breath. "Space is a luxury," he agrees.

"So is a nice smell."

"Wet leaves," he smiles.

"Mmm," Leili says, "Rain is in the air."

"Soon," agrees Hooman.

Leili pauses to look at a villa set far enough off the road for privacy but close enough to give a sense of habitation—close enough for the large picture windows to light up and frame other lives in the dark.

"Is this your neighborhood?" Leili teases.

"Nope, I'm even further up the mountains with the new bourgeoisie. You know those crazy Persian palaces?"

"Faux terra-cotta-colored concrete monstrosities with stoic

columns and Romanesque statuettes, twelve-foot French doors and impermeable wrought-iron gates?"

"Yup," Hooman laughs.

"You're kidding?"

"I am. That's where Nima lives."

"No? He's not the type."

"You haven't met his mom."

Leili thinks about her own neighborhood where the nouveau-Bazzaris keep building more and more into the sides of the mountains while what used to be neighborhoods are becoming business districts. Her street was filled with families when she was a child and now it's a mix of old apartments and new government offices.

"In my neighborhood curtains are always drawn, blinds are closed and the ugly grey highrises reflect back the city."

"Or worse, one's own reflection," Hooman laughs.

"Look." She points to a large villa set back from the road. It has a sliding glass door with filmy curtains and walking shadows.

"They must trust their neighbors."

"What neighbors?" Hooman laughs. "The trees?"

"The stillness." The dark feels safe and in the quiet there's a sense of life that is lost in the crowds only a mile south.

"I feel safer in crowds," Hooman says. "I like to see exactly where people are. People are better behaved in crowds."

"You think?"

"Let's go! We're going to be late." Hooman picks up his pace.

"Is it a show? Where are you taking me?" Leili asks Hooman's back as she runs after him up the empty road where spruce branches softly brush dew kisses along her sleeve as she passes.

Hooman stops at a warped wooden gate just before the Darband turnoff. He taps out a short rhythm with the brass knocker and waits. He motions for Leili to stay silent and whispers, "Once we pass through the gate we cannot speak again until we come back out, OK? Imagine this as a prolonged meditation."

Leili nods.

Footsteps crush leaves and slosh through puddles as they come closer. A chain clinks and the wooden gate creaks open. A man in his mid-thirties, with a long beard, jeans and a black turtleneck and baggy black pants greets them with his right hand to his heart and a short bow. Neither he nor Hooman speaks. The man smiles at Leili and motions for them to come inside the garden.

The three of them slosh through puddles toward an old brown brick villa with a large veranda guarded by stone lions. The villa is dimly lit in the distance, which suggests that a caretaker, perhaps this man, has only lit the minimal amount of lights to keep away thieves. Leili wonders if the house, with its aura of former majesty and unusually large grounds, was abandoned after the Revolution.

Raindrops begin and softly match the faint rhythm of their footsteps—tapping, then dancing and finally flooding the gutters. They just make it under the rafters of the veranda when a rush of rain is released from the heavens to conceal them from the world outside. Hooman squeezes Leili's hand.

The foyer is silent and empty save for a crowd of men's shoes that jam the entry as at a mosque. An ornate crystal chandelier faintly illuminates a wall of jackets that hang from a row of hooks. Musical instrument cases are placed on benches and against walls.

A double door is opened to a circle of thirty or more men, young and old, who sit cross-legged in the center of a large room with intricate mirror work reminiscent of eighteenth-century Persia. Tambours and *daf*s are at the ready on their laps. Their eyes are closed and their heads bent down in what looks like prayer. The security of the silence and warmth of the warm orange light envelops them. A border of black soot that separates the high yellowing ceiling from the walls suggests long candlelit nights. Shiny maplewood floors reflect the two fireplaces on either end of the room. The only furnishing is an enormous antique Persian rug woven with the tree-of-life motif.

Hooman leads Leili to the corner near a fireplace, just outside the circle of men, and motions for her to sit down next to him.

"It's a *khanegah*, Sufi lodge," he says and closes his eyes.

The gentle tapping of the rain outside blends seamlessly with the men's meditative breathing inside. Leili settles into herself and closes her eyes.

The room takes a long collective inhale that is released in tandem with the sound of tambours that come in all at once. The unanticipated tambours, the intensity of their number, the beauty of their synchronicity catches in the center of Leili's chest. She exhales. No sooner does she settle into the rhythm of the tambours, then the dafs come in like a wave. They rush toward her with the power of the ocean. She is under water and surrounded, protected, fluid, breathing. She has gills; it is the opposite of drowning. The dafs change rhythm and she is above water again, floating, buoyant.

She wants to open her eyes, to look, to memorize this moment. But she keeps them closed and tries to see in a different, unfamiliar way—imprinting without camera, pen, paper, or paint. And then the familiar desire to create or to memorize gives way to something else: a moment she wants to sink into and stay in, to just be. She imagines herself becoming part of the rhythm—jumping into the fire and becoming one with the heat. With closed eyes she sees the men's peaceful faces. She is in love with each and every expression, with every beautiful closed mouth and with every gnarl of the tambour's walnut wood. She falls into a trance just as the dafs chase the tambours into a new rhythm.

Mouths make circles and chant one of Allah's 99 names: hu, hu, hu, hu . . . Leili wants to stand, to jump, and to go outside and scream. At the same time she knows she is immobile and that ultimately she never wants to leave. Her head is back; her eyes are closed. She sways like the soft spruce branches that cast their shadows along the windows.

The dafs diminish—softer, slower. The tambours become quieter and quieter. The swaying smolders like the dying embers—their light slowly fading from orange to pink behind closed eyelids, until all is still.

Hooman's knee touches her knee and she freezes, afraid that her slightest motion might change the direction of his desire.

Leili opens her eyes. The fire has burned down. Faces are obscured and heads are silhouettes against the mirrored walls in the dimming light. One by one the men stand. Holding their instruments to their heart they bow to their fellows and then turn around and bow to the fire before walking out into the hall. When everyone has left the salon, Hooman stands and waits for Leili. She looks up at him and like the robe of a dervish that falls to the floor something in Leili falls away.

They bow to the fire and back away until they are in the hallway where dafs are covered and the tambours are tenderly placed on their sides in velvet cases. Overcoats are donned in silence. When it is his turn, the dervish kisses the cheeks of the man next to him, puts his hand to his heart, and bows before walking out the door. The last one bows to Leili. No one speaks, except to say, *Ya haqq*, Oh truth.

There is a pattern to their leaving. One, and then two, maybe another man, and then another three. Hooman knows instinctively when to take leave. He motions to Leili and they bow together on cue.

Hooman calls, "Ya haqq."

Halfway down the mountain Hooman pauses, takes Leili's hand, leans in and kisses her. The rain falls harder and harder, louder and louder.

He kisses her wet forehead. "Will you come to my place?" he asks.

"You have a place?"

"It's a long story. It's a bookstore. Will you?"

"Now?" Leili asks.

"No, in two weeks, on Chahar Shanbeh Soori—for the night?" He blushes. Leili smiles. She's never seen him blush. "We can meet there after practice. The city will be on fire—no one will even notice us." He gives her an earnest look. "You don't have to answer me now."

بسم الله الرحمن الرحيم

In the Name of God

Walter Benjamin, I love him. He says in "The Storyteller," "The art of storytelling is coming to an end. Less and less frequently do we encounter people with the ability to tell a tale properly. More and more often there is embarrassment all around when the wish to hear a story is expressed. It is as if something that seemed inalienable to us, the securest among our possessions, were taken from us: the ability to exchange experiences."

Benjamin was ahead of his time. His ghost lingers, waiting for us to move on while he waits us out in purgatory. We should release the poor soul.

Exchange of experiences, I like that. Our theater will work against all of the identity building that was forced on us after the Revolution, all of the work that went into making us obedient Islamic men and women where the highest goal was to sacrifice ourselves for the collective, for the nation, quite literally through martyrdom or giving up a family member.

Our theater must be therapy. But how? Certainly not like some popular neorealist cinema that redefines and revitalizes our national identity (especially for the West) by showing pretty landscapes and little kids that could be from any Caucasian country in the Asian Steppes, losing balloons and shoes on their way to a new life. Ours must be for Iranians, by Iranians—for both the actor and the audience. Our sacrifice will be the intense physicality of our performance—the great physical demand from the body of the actor. It's a different kind of martyrdom.

Practice must be painful and continue until the body is fragmented and destroyed (think Vienna Actionists, Grotowski, Butoh Theater). The body is broken down, but the soul takes flight. This is not like martyrdom during our war where mysticism was a union with God through death. But a mysticism where we meet God on earth: in a blade of grass, a tree, a piece of trash and ultimately in ourselves.

We have to stop feeling bad about ourselves because we have aspirations that are different.

Making the theater about therapy rather than about entertainment is getting really intense. Agha Jerzy has no problem with it. He says, "We demand it from the actors . . . something extreme . . . something very definite that reaches beyond the meaning of 'theatre' and is more like an act of living and way of existence."

Drama is so powerful. Art is so powerful. "All efforts to render politics aesthetic culminate in one thing: war," says Benjamin. We could also say that war makes politics aesthetic. We need to fight this on a visual front. A visual affront.

At the heart of a good story is the ability to create a visual. And yet, too many images can be damaging. A word-image, poetry . . . keeps a story alive long after we're done reading. We close our eyes and the words fade, but the visual trace stays. Is this why Plato distrusted poetry? Khomeini was a Platonist: he both distrusted and made deft use of visuals. Martyrdom needs an audience.

Tehran Burning

Hooman walks to the center. "Take your positions." He tells them that there will always be an element of fear on the stage. "The performance is an opportunity to overcome fear. What you don't deal with one night presents an opportunity for the next night."

The scene is supposed to open with Kamran in center stage, but he hasn't shown up.

"Take Kamran's place," Hooman tells Nima.

Leili takes her position in front of Nima, and raises her arms. Nima steps back and Leili arches her head, her arms and her back toward him as he moves away from her. The movement ends with her in a backward bridge arch, her fingers near Nima's toes but not touching.

"More expression, Leili. You are unfolding yourself toward him: with every step he takes back, your every breath moves you closer to him—but you cannot reach him. He wants you to reach him. His expression is pained and he longs for you."

Nima gives Hooman a quizzical look. "Where's all his passion coming from?"

"This is about a relationship with yourself and not with each other. You will need each other for support in your lifts, as spotters for falls; you must trust one another one hundred percent."

Leili places her lower back on the ground, tries to lift her core and collapses.

"Such a martyr, Leili," Arezoo quips.

"This is hardly martyrdom, Arezoo." Hooman's words are stern. Both women startle and turn around to look at him.

"Let's get back to practice," Hooman says, taking Leili's arm and pulling her into the center of the room.

"Hey, no touching," she says and mock slaps his wrist.

Arezoo glances at Nima and raises her brows.

"Ok, we need lighter movements; your muscles are developing to lift you, not to ground you . . . Light," Hooman whispers into the candlelit silence.

"Light is hardly what I feel: I'm heavy, tired, clumsy," Nima says.

Hooman doesn't respond. He walks around them silently correcting postures, sometimes standing and looking, other times crouching down, examining.

Nima bends forward, tucks his chin into his neck and neatly, compactly and gently tumbles into a perfect ball. Leili flinches when the back of his neck hits the ground.

They all exhale when Nima rolls right into a standing position. Leili, excited, raises her hands to clap, and then remembers where she is and stops herself.

Nima walks over to Hooman and asks, "What, now that you don't smoke anymore, we don't get breaks?"

Hooman smiles down at the floor.

"You're under a new influence," Nima teases him. "Don't give me that look, Hooman. You can't act as well as we can." He laughs.

Hooman moves back into the middle of the circle and says, "We're done for today. Nima and I are going to soundproof this place the first day of the Nowruz break. The paint is toxic, so we won't be able to practice in here for a few days. Please keep up the work at home."

"Wait," Nima calls out, as they're about to depart.

"Shhh," Leili admonishes him.

"It's Chahar Shanbeh Soori . . . and we have candles. We have to jump!" Nima exclaims.

Arezoo beams. "So true," she agrees.

Nima lines up the candles.

The fireworks are already crackling through the night sky above them. The smell of burning bales of hay all over the city already permeates the air and with it a sense of excitement.

"Wonder whether they're arresting folks this year or letting us be?" Nima jokes.

"Hmmm . . . election year, my bet is on arresting," Arezoo offers.

"Hurry, then," Leili says.

"It's OK," Hooman reassures her. She blushes when she meets his eye.

"What's the hurry?" Arezoo asks.

Leili ignores her.

Nima grabs Arezoo's hand and pulls her. "Just jump," he says, leading her over the candles.

Before Leili was tall enough to run and jump on her own, her father would bundle her in his arms and leap across the row of burning hay piles in the park, their yard, garden or street. She felt so safe then, against the fire's glow, wrapped in her father's arms.

"Take my yellow, burned-out embers and give me your red energy," they whisper to the fire as they jump.

Even Hooman, who rarely joins them, makes his symbolic leap into the New Year. He's the first to leave.

"It's your turn to lock up," he says and tosses the keys to Nima.

Outside, the air is smoky and the night lights up in random patches of orange and white. Leili makes her way past revelers calling to her to jump. "Come on," a young man yells, "Don't be scared—what's the hurry?"

Things are quieter on Revolution Street and almost deserted by the time she reaches the bookstore where Hooman is waiting inside.

"Anyone out there?" he asks.

"Not really."

Hooman lowers the store's metal shutters. He locks the glass door behind him and turns off the light over the cash register.

"Follow closely," he says. "It's just like descending into the theater." He feels his way down the backstairs of the store in the dark. The temperature drops, and the humidity increases with each clanking step down into the cool calm beneath the city.

"Wow," Leili exclaims when Hooman twists a single 60-watt bulb that hangs from a nest of exposed electrical wires and reveals a storeroom of floor-to-ceiling books.

"My own private Alexandria."

"Is it really yours?"

"No, I work here. We sell the usual permissible books in the front and provide our trusted customers with used, out of-print and illegally printed books in the basement. My job is to fill the banned book orders from the basement at night."

"Just you?"

"Just me, puffing away on my pipe, working away in this musty protectorate of books and buildings."

"Must be the lack of air. You're quite poetic down here," Leili jokes.

"It's the company," he says. "Coffee?" Hooman offers and motions for her to sit on the thin mattress laid-out against a wall of books.

"Is this . . . ," she starts to say but stops cold when an unmistakable step is heard from overhead.

Hooman quickly twists the light off. The wires sizzle and burn his fingers.

Pure silence. Even the books hold their breath.

"Door's locked," he whispers.

"Shhh." Leili presses herself against the wall and looks around.

"Stairway is the only exit," Hooman says, reading her mind.

After what feels like hours, Hooman whispers, "I'm going to go look. We can't sit frozen like this all night. Stay here."

Leili grabs his sleeve.

"Shhh, let go, it's OK," he says and leaves.

"All clear," Hooman calls down.

Leili runs up the stairs before he has a chance to come down. The only light in the store seeps in through the metal shutters from the street, but it's enough to see the bookshelves, the counter, and Hooman's figure.

"I'm scared," Leili says. He takes her in his arms.

"You're shaking," she says.

"I haven't felt this queasy since the day my mother left me at school." He forces a laugh.

"You never talk about her," Leili says, looking up at him in the dark. "Where is she?"

"Mashhad."

He pulls her over to the counter, where they sit on the floor with their backs against the wall.

"It's a religious city," Leili says.

"Spiritual," he corrects her. "I grew up there."

"I didn't know that."

"I haven't visited my family since I came to Tehran for school seven years ago."

"Don't you miss them? They must miss you like crazy," Leili says.

"It's just me and my mom and she's a little crazy. It's painful to see her."

"Why?"

"She's in a convalescent home." Hooman pauses. "The doctors think she's lost her mind. They treat her as if she's lost all her feelings and memories, too."

"A mother remembers. She must have her child memorized somewhere deep in her cells," Leili insists.

"Maybe it's better that she doesn't know that I live in a bookstore basement sleeping with the royalist bourgeois William Shakespeare and the evil atheist Robert Graves."

"Where'd you learn the language of the Great Satan, anyway?"

"English lessons at Madam Mary's language school. Every Saturday morning my mom dressed me in the same little hand-me-down burgundy suit and dropped me off with the bourgeoisie. I'd look back at her and she looked so scared but determined. Her determination kept me from running back to her or crying."

"Where was your father?"

"Away," Hooman says to the dark.

The floor creaks. Leili loosens her grip on him and straightens up. "Hooman, I'm scared," Leili says.

Hooman pulls her back and holds her tighter. "You should go. I'm not sure that it's safe here anymore."

"What about you? Where will you go?"

"I'll be OK."

Hooman walks her out the door and helps her find a taxi in the mess of smoke and ashes that the street has become.

In the morning Leili returns to the bookstore on her way to school to look for Hooman, but the metal grate is still down and locked. She waits a few minutes and then leaves.

Later, Hooman tells her that there was no sign of a break-in at the bookstore in the morning but when he returned in the evening to go to work it was completely shuttered.

"I looked around. Then I swear I heard someone say, 'It has

closed its eyes to the world. I wouldn't ask around if I were you.'
I turned, but no one was there."

"Could it have been your imagination?"

"We both heard those steps last night. And, there was a lit cigarette smoldering on the ground."

"Hooman . . ."

بسم الله الرحمن الرحيم

In the Name of God

It's cold and dark out there. I feel safest underground: the riskiest place in Tehran has become the safest place in Tehran. Sometimes I want to stay here after practice, lie down and take a nap with Leili standing near, watching over me. We are little night owls . . . hu hu . . . do owls know that they're repeating one of God's ninety-nine names? Tonight is the solstice, the beginning of spring. The owls have their own Zikr tonight while we mortal mystics find our own ways to commune with God.

Oh God, what will I translate without the bookstore? Time to start making stuff up, time to turn to fiction.

Have I kept too much of myself from my actors? What have I missed? What have I allowed to happen by making this space, by nurturing it? Agha Jerzy says, "Respect for autonomy means enormous demands." The actor's freedom comes from the plentitude of the guide; any lack "implies imposition, dictatorship . . ."

I may have tried to be the opposite of a dictator—but all hell seems to have broken loose, regardless.

Limbs rise and fall one after the other like waves. A breath is released; a limb goes limp, softly, silently, suppressing any note of anguish, of inner revolt. Admitting to pain could cause the collective resolve to float out the peephole in the roof with their tired exhales, and so they suffer in silence.

Every breath is valuable. Every breath moves the chest toward the sky, toward the heavens. Every breath is as strong as a muscle.

We're doing breathing and movement exercises, but not the vocals. Agha Jerzy has no idea how free he really was, Stalin or no Stalin. It's hell not to be able to use sound.

Second day of Nowruz
Space . . . how much physical space do we allow between another and ourselves? Permission . . . how much permission do we need between another and ourselves? Freedom . . . how much freedom do we get in order to decide?

Leili is less scared. Kamran is less arrogant. Kamran won't struggle with his soul in the same way; for all his vanity, he is at home in himself, he doesn't need to expand. Leili needs to learn how to take space; he needs to learn how to give it; Arezoo needs to learn how to share it. And Nima—thank you, God, for Nima—a human form of humility.

In our little pit there's no place for fear or pride or exhaustion. These feelings come later: at home sitting alone in a favorite chair, lying in bed, relaxing in a hot Epsom salt bath and reflecting on what happened during the day. Every subterranean minute is used productively. The candles flicker, the city rolls on and Tehran's pollution hovers over the peephole like a lover with bad breath. I love the sound of their weight crushing the cardboard beneath them, their little gasps of pain and effort. It's so productive, so real—like a dancer's caught breath that slips out during a performance. Their reasons for wanting to run and a stronger desire to stay, fold together, and then open cautiously like a large fan maneuvered by small delicate fingers.

I wonder if Arezoo is practicing somewhere else as well. When she pulls up her sleeves, her arms look muscular, scratched-up and scabbed. She's never been hurt on my watch.

Arezoo . . . Like a sculptor with his putty, I'm playing with her. It's fun. Her face becomes a blank slate, her arms dangle limply alongside her body, her fingers spread like webbing. Her chest and shoulders protrude forward into the future before her legs are ready to take her there. Her

body arcs over Kamran's and he places his hands on her waist and pro-
pels her to a place of rest.

Leili has caught her in a photo smiling. The candlelight softens her,
makes her look more peaceful—beautiful.

War Paint

During the break Leili runs into Nima, Kamran and Arezoo outside the university library.

"Looks like we're all cramming over the break," Leili says, laughing.

"Not really. It's just a safe meeting spot. We're going to play paintball. Want to come?" Nima asks.

"Seriously? She can barely do a handstand," Kamran protests before she can answer.

"Yes," Leili says, in spite of Kamran.

"You have no idea what paintball is, do you?" Arezoo laughs.

"Not really," Leili admits.

"How fun," Arezoo says.

After listening to a description of what sounds like a bunch of boys ambushing each other in fake bushes with paint, Leili says, "I'll just watch."

"That's not an option; players only on the field," Nima says. "I'm a member of the club and I know the owner. He'll let you try for free."

"You guys are all members?"

"Just me and Kamran," Nima says.

"Hooman?"

"Are you kidding? He'd never join a club," Arezoo says.

"Or wear camouflage," Kamran adds laughing.

"He's not so into guns either," Leili agrees.

"They're not guns; they're markers. But Hooman did say that he thinks it's a good theater exercise," says Nima.

"Yeah, it allows a rush without killing."

"Not true. He says the only reason the government allows it is because it's training future soldiers at our own expense."

The manager hands Leili a heavy camouflage jumpsuit to pull over her rupush, a protective helmet to wear over her russari, a belt with pellets of paint and what looks like a machine gun, but which everyone insists on calling a marker.

"Dressing rooms over there." The man points to the corner of an abandoned video arcade where Arezoo is already pulling her jumpsuit over her tight jeans and skimpy V-neck t-shirt.

Leili joins Arezoo. "You took off your rupush," Leili comments.

"I don't want to wrinkle it," Arezoo answers.

"Here, you need these." Nima runs over to the women and hands Leili a pair of goggles. Arezoo shows her how to dump the pellets into her marker and they walk out into what looks like a Hollywood set.

"It's so quiet," Leili remarks.

"That'll end. There are about fifty people on their way. We're early. Let's go to the operations room and meet the team."

The operations room is only one of 32 rooms and hiding places in the 2700 square meter indoor field covered in sand imported from the Caspian Sea and outfitted with artificial trenches and suspension bridges. The "coach" outlines an elaborate tactic to capture the other team's flag and then they're off, at first in ones and twos. Then, suddenly, the place is crawling with people and paint.

It's only a game, and yet the fear of being hit, the hiding, the chasing and being chased, and the loud sound of pellets hitting and exploding drive Leili to jump into a ditch for shelter some distance from the main play. A few minutes later, a man jumps in with her.

"I'm wearing green," she says. Green tells him she's a woman and that he can't touch her.

"Sorry, was about to get hit," he says and is off, leaving Leili with a little tingle of excitement. She's still catching her breath when another player in green rolls in, panting.

Leili leans over her. "Are you OK?" she asks.

"Leili?"

"Shadi?"

"I haven't seen you in ages. What classes are you taking? Have I seen you in any of our prereqs? New friends?" she asks, still out of breath. She sits up and looks at Leili through speckled goggles.

"Sort of, we have a school project together," Leili lies.

"What class?"

"Theater."

"You're taking a theater class? Is that even allowed for electrical majors?"

"Must have slipped by . . . and you? I didn't know you did this."

"My boyfriend is a paintball champ. His team won Moscow last year. He was over here a second ago . . . looking for me, I think . . ."

"Boyfriend?" And just as the word is out of her mouth, Leili is pelted with fluorescent green goop.

"I've wanted to do that for months!" Kamran laughs as he runs away.

Leili presses her cheek against the cold window of the taxi and watches the empty traffic squares with their dry fountains and fading Revolutionary murals pass in a muted blur toward the mountains and home. She vaguely regrets turning down Shadi for pizza after paintball, but she just wasn't in the mood to explain her new life. Ghostly steam escapes from the cracks in the splintering wood door of an old bakery—and Leili makes a mental note to buy bread along the way.

بسم الله الرحمن الرحيم

In the Name of God

I've always wanted to experiment with Gestalt psychology, where they push and prod and push until there's a breakthrough. Where a person reaches her absolute, exhausted limit, at a place where there is no energy to keep up appearances and all defenses are down. But I've never had the nerve to ask them to stay all night. Besides, if they did, their defenses on the contrary would be higher than ever.

But am I not pushing them enough? Gestalt would say push; otherwise we become our own captors. And maybe we already are? We walk about our practice room as if on constant tiptoe, listening for and waiting to be caught, and I wonder are we doing anything worthy of being caught? We should at least push if we're taking this risk. If they catch us together they'll assume the worst, so why not do the worst?

The great overseers of strict Islamic morals say women are not allowed to sing for anyone but other women. I'm just like them, censoring Arezoo. The worst effect of oppressive regimes is we do their work for them. Time to let Arezoo scream?

I've been thinking that if she can't sing then we'll damn well redefine singing. We're like junk collectors in the bowels of censorship . . . searching for our voices in the debris and only finding silence.

Another rainy night . . .
In Nezami Ganjavi's tale, Leili and Majnun, *Leili was promised to a prince and so Majnun spent years wandering the desert, writing poems lamenting his lost love. Travelers who heard him in the desert carried*

his poetry through the sand and caravanserais to Leili's window. One night, Leili slipped out to meet Majnun in the desert. When she stood before him in all her beauty, after all those months of separation, Majnun fainted. Leili's image was singed in his imagination and so her physical touch destroyed the mirage.

Has she already become a figment of my imagination?

It's like a character that you create from a real person—once you put them in fiction it's hard to see them again. You feel queasy, uneasy, and unreal. So what can be seen and what can't be shown?

I was looking through a stack of Leili's recent photos and one slipped out of the pile. She tried to take it back; it was of a man's hand, gripping a pen. It was my pen, my hand and my essence that she had captured and taken from me in her photo.

Equinox

The still-cold spring breeze tickles Leili's uncovered head as she leans out of her window. Lightning over the mountains exposes shocks of craggy peaks and leaning trees in nature's stormy darkroom. The city changes in the rain. Leili becomes philosophical and in the mood to read when it rains. Her pores are open to new ideas as she listens for distant thunder in the mountains and imagines Hooman meditating under the gathering clouds. She wonders if he is already in Darband, waiting. He told her to meet him at the hiker statue in Darband on Thursday.

She shuts the window and does a quick scan of her parents' bookshelf and sees that if she wants to read anything other than Marxist manifestos, photography manuals or Saqi's Danielle Steel romances, she will have to leave the comfort of the dry apartment.

"I'm off to Niavaran," Leili calls to her mother.

"Where to?" Saqi walks into the den.

"The bookstore."

"It's Nowruz. Everything's closed."

"Right, I forgot."

"Here, read this—it's great," Saqi says and pulls a thick paperback off the shelf.

Leili glances at the sensationalizing blurb on the back of the book: "Wealthy, educated woman leaves her upstanding family to marry a calloused carpenter—can the inevitable heartache a century ago be any different today?"

"It was a huge hit."

"I remember." In cafés and at friends' parties the fate of the book's pathetic heroine was hotly debated. Friends fell on both sides of the divide. Romantics applauded the bravery and self-lessness of a young woman who gave up her place in society, not to mention a fortune, to marry for love while realists found her naïve and deserving of the misery that ensued as the result of a "stupid decision and a bad marriage," as Saqi put it when she finished reading it.

Leili listlessly throws the book on the couch and falls down next to it. Her eyes feel heavy after only a chapter and so she pulls a wool throw over her head for an afternoon nap just as Saqi walks back in and demands, "Why aren't you dressed?"

"I am dressed. Are we going somewhere?" Leili asks.

Saqi is dressed in her visiting clothes—a tight-fitting navy skirt that accentuates every curve from her abdomen to her knees and a silk blouse that bellows like a sail from her bosom to her belt. She has baby-blue eye shadow on that was popular in the seventies when she bought it and coral pink lipstick.

"Nowruz visitors," she says hopefully.

Leili gives her mother a quizzical look. They haven't had Nowruz visitors in years and her parents rarely make Nowruz visits outside. Saqi might amble across the street to Sefat's with cookies and flowers, dragging Leili along for her New Year's coffee fortune, but that would be the extent of her visits out.

Leili wishes it were already the third day of Nowruz when the city will be quiet and they can stop pretending to wait for visitors. The obligatory Nowruz visits consist of younger family members visiting older family members (of which none remain in Leili's family—they've either died or migrated) and then old friends (they too either died prematurely in prison for their political views or escaped) and then the newly married (also obsolete, given the lack of the former). In the past Leili would at last escape their silent apartment for the Caspian to Shadi's family villa. She hasn't told Saqi that she's spent most of this year underground with a new group of friends and has lost touch with her old friends and that she wasn't invited to the Caspian this year, because the little omission will allow her to spend the night with Hooman.

The rest of the afternoon passes in silence. The smell of freshly baked coffeecake made for possible visitors that never materialize taunts Leili until finally it fades into the smell of fried onions.

Leili finds Saqi cooking dinner.

"You've changed your clothes," Leili says lightly.

Saqi doesn't answer her. She ambles to the refrigerator and pulls out another cutlet, unwraps it, and places it in the frying pan.

"I forgot to buy pickles, but we have tomatoes if you like?" She doesn't look up from the frying pan, where onions turn from translucent to brown.

"Would you like me to slice them?" Leili asks.

"I already have. They're on the table."

Leili walks over to hug her mother when the doorbell rings.

Saqi and Leili look at each other and then at their clothes.

"We'd better hurry and change," Saqi says with a new vitality.

"Could be a delivery," Leili says.

"Run to the intercom," Saqi suggests as she wipes her hands on her apron, takes it off swiftly and heads toward her bedroom.

Leili picks up the intercom receiver. "It's Sefat, open up!"

Leili buzzes her in.

"What a surprise." Leili kisses Sefat on both of her chubby rouged cheeks.

Sefat looks Leili over and says, "Hmmm, so grown up." She clucks with approval.

"Where's Saqi? I brought fresh ground coffee from Villa." Sefat looks around as she slips her russari off her head. She almost never wears a rupush; her dress is as large and blustery as a tent and pretty much covers everything.

"How nice of you," Saqi says, greeting Sefat and taking the coffee. "I've missed you." Saqi takes Sefat's arm and leads her into the salon, where they never sit.

"Nice rugs, silk." Sefat admires the elegant Kashan carpets. "A wonderful room for a wedding." She winks at Leili. "The place can easily seat sixty," Sefat concludes.

"Tea?" Leili asks.

"Coffee!" Saqi and Sefat exclaim in unison.

"Three coffees." Sefat winks at Leili.

"I'll make it," Saqi says and retreats to the kitchen.

Sefat studies the dining room.

"I've never been in here," she says.

"No one has," Leili says.

Since the Revolution the couches and chairs have been covered in their own makeshift chadors, guarding them from dust, the possibility of a party and from anyone who wishes to loiter there alone–something Saqi strongly discourages. Once her father's friends began being picked up for their political views and sent off to jail, parties seemed pointless and like an affront to their memory, so the room remains a relic of a past Leili barely experienced. It is the first room that is cleaned for the New Year and the last place they ever sit—save for tonight.

"My, you look so grown up," Sefat beams.

Leili blushes. "Changed," Sefat declares. "We haven't done a cup reading in a long time."

Saqi appears with a tray of tiny espresso cups on saucers and a mound of Nowruz cookies: *noon berenji*, made from rose water and rice flour, *nokhod-chi* made from chickpeas and cardamom and *bamieh*, fried dough dripping in honey.

Sefat takes one of each and then delicately sips her coffee. Saqi downs her coffee and turns the saucer for a fortune.

"Leili?" Sefat prods when Leili places her cup upright on her saucer. "You're not trying to hide anything, are you?" Sefat leans over and pinches Leili's thigh.

"Of course not," Leili says and takes the cup and turns it over defiantly.

Sefat bends over and reaches for her handbag with some effort. She finds her reading glasses and perches them on her bulbous nose. She picks up Leili's cup, takes a look inside and says, "Weather's meant to be a bit chilly in the Caspian this year."

Leili stands abruptly. "You have to see our *Haft Sin*."

"Leili?" Saqi is exasperated.

"You have a Haft Sin?" Sefat asks, placing Leili's cup back on the tray.

"Why so surprised?" Saqi asks. "Leili and I prepare our Nowruz Haft Sin well in advance of the equinox. From the time she was a child Leili loved the smell of the fermenting soybeans, watching them sprout and grow bigger and bigger day by day." Saqi smiles at Leili, takes her hand and pulls her back down on the couch next to her. "By the time the Nowruz goldfish begin to appear in the markets, we already have ours at home. Leili even has one in her room, ready to take to the Caspian with her this year." Saqi beams.

"Really?" Sefat says. She shifts her behemoth frame in her little seat and readjusts her reading glasses. "So," she takes Leili's cup and peers back in. "I'm just starting to see a pattern."

When Sefat finally leaves, the house reverts to its natural silence and calm. "Your father's not hungry," Saqi tells Leili as they set the table in the kitchen for dinner.

Saqi studies Leili as she eats. "You've lost weight; your new clothes are already baggy."

"I guess," Leili answers. She looks up expectantly.

The odd nicety, the simple question—Leili wills her mother to

pry deeper. If Saqi only pushed a little, Leili would tell her everything: about the theater, about slowly changing her major, about
Hooman.

But Saqi only says, "I missed Sefat. It was nice of her to come.
And what a reading! Seems your Nowruz trip this year is a mo-
mentous one." Saqi beams.

Leili's never really lied to her before now, not like this. She's
not sure she knows how. "Yes," she says, careful not to meet her
mother's eyes.

Saqi stops eating and looks tenderly at her daughter.

"I'm tired. I should get off to bed," Leili says.

"You barely ate. You've been so hungry lately. Why not today?"

"I didn't get any exercise today," Leili answers absently.

"Oh, so that's it. You have been exercising. Why didn't you
tell me? I thought you seemed . . ." Her mother looks at her ap-
provingly and says, "different."

"I met some friends who like to swim," Leili lies more easily
now. Her mother brightens.

"You should've said," Saqi sighs with relief. "I wondered, all
those late nights . . ."

"Yes, women get the pool after hours. I didn't want you to
think that I'm wasting money." Leili looks away from her mother's proud stare.

Saqi heaves herself up, goes to the dresser and takes out an
envelope and hands it to Leili.

"Your Nowruz gift," she says.

Leili kisses her, and looks in the envelope at one thousand US
dollars.

"Why?" Leili gasps.

"Just in case. Sefat said you might need it. Keep it somewhere
safe. Hide it." Leili slips the envelope in her pocket and goes to
hug her mother, who is already at the sink and elbowdeep in
warm sudsy dishes.

"Good night," Saqi says. Leili passes her father in the hallway on her way to her room.

"Is it safe?" he asks, looking around nervously.

Leili laughs, gives him a peck on his cheek and answers, "Yes. She left ages ago."

Before climbing into her bed she taps a dusting of food into the bowl of the bulbous orange New Year's goldfish she's bought for Hooman. She glances at her wall clock and counts the hours until she'll lift his glass bowl off the dresser and walk away with him in her arms.

بسم الله الرحمن الرحيم

In the Name of God

The weight their life had then, the contours and shapes of their bodies and the impression they left on the snowy world dissipated forever.

A forensic anthropologist or an archeologist takes the outline of a skeleton, the remains, and then fills it in with imaginary flesh and a story. If they can do it, why can't I? A book—made of imaginary flesh based on years of reading and an educated guess—an educated play.

I can't do it because I'm not privy to people's private lives: the in-between moments, the ones that are less dramatic but that count for far more than we ever give them credit for, and the incubating moments, the quiet ones that become the meat of a good story, that lead to the final action, that build character. Those are the moments that elude me. And yet those are the moments that might ultimately explain why my character does what she did. I know how she handled the big drama. But how did she handle those little moments?

How do we show love in a censored world? How can we write about it in a journal? As allegory? Myth?
Mystical allegories about the separation of the beloved and the lover say distance generates desire. I've been thinking a lot about mystical separation, desire . . . loneliness in a city of millions.

It was freezing tonight. I walked alone past the pastry shops, slipper stores and flower stands. Little boys peddling coupons grabbed at my sleeves—well-meaning women shooed them away.

I passed by a little sidewalk park with a fountain, under which a man sits every night, his face covered with a newspaper, a hat placed in front of him, waiting for change. I stared at the newspaper as if it were his face. Text, news of the day, black dripping ink stared back at me where there should have been a fleshy face. He covers his shame with the news, with the anonymity of the affairs of the world that he is so much a part of but which makes him just another faceless being on the Tehran streets. Poverty is worse than a veil; you can't see its eyes. To be an activist and obsessed with the veil is to look the other way. I dropped him a few coins and then shamelessly looked away. But the faceless man stays with me like a lover who is photographed against the sun. Neither leaves a realistic impression, but both leave an unerasable trace—more cutting and closer to truth than would a sharper image.

I do the only thing I can with him—I turn him into a character.

Fig Leaves

Sycamores stand sentry all along Vali Asr Avenue as they have
since the day of the Shah's coronation parade over forty years
ago when the street was called Pahlavi Avenue. That was before
the Revolution, before Leili was born, before any memory could
form of the things that disappeared: fresh air, large walled-in
gardens, outdoor cafés and the breeze on a woman's neck. She
only knows what remained: the snowcapped Alborz mountains, the sycamore, willow and sarv trees and the wide-open
joobs that run along Vali Asr Avenue, from the posh northern
end of the city where they are fed by melting mountain snow
to the poor south, taking along the way leaves, cigarette butts,
plastic Pofak wrappers, scraps of lost poetry, unwanted fortunes and phone numbers surreptitiously penned in bleeding
ink on the backs of matchbooks and gum wrappers. Leili even
spots tiny castaway Nowruz goldfish, some floating with the
current, others against it, their little golden backs winking up at
her in the sunlight.

Slipping her hand into her rupush's pocket, she feels for the
scrap of poetry from the mountain divinator, rubs it for luck and
steps out onto the street to flag down a shared cab.

Leili spots Hooman as her taxi climbs up the mountain road.
Fear and excitement ride every nerve in her body as she watches
each of his feet fall to the pavement like an exclamation mark. Is
this the speed of desire, or the speed of escape? She turns her face

from the window and takes a long deep breath, exhales, and asks the taxi to pull over.

"Hooman?" she breathes, catching up to him.

She walks alongside him, almost touching.

"Risky, speaking to a man you're not related to," he jokes, looking straight ahead, pretending not to know her, but smiling.

"Do we need provisions?" she asks.

"Just you." He looks at her, smiles and says, "And apparently a goldfish."

She shivers. He takes off his jacket and offers it to her. She hugs the bowl tighter and says, "I'll be fine once we start climbing."

"In that case," he says, putting his jacket back on and relieving her of the goldfish bowl, "Let's move."

He walks quickly ahead of her, past the giant hiker statue, in the direction of the hills.

He looks over his shoulder and smiles at her. She is panting behind him. She passes him. They pretend to be strangers until they are halfway up the mountain where the path is less worn from flocks of day-trippers, where people fall away from the path into the little garden cafés, where the tenor of nearby conversations slows and softens with the surrounding silence. After Hajji's restaurant the only sound is that of the rushing waterfall beneath them.

"It may be a bit slippery from last night's rain." He takes her hand and leads her across the bridge where they first met.

They stop at a tributary off the mountain path. It's one of a few on the way up the mountain that lead to large orchards and summer homes.

"Walk ahead. It gets a little narrow here, we have to walk single file."

"We're going off the main path," Leili comments.

"Watch out for donkeys," Hooman calls to her.

She turns to face him, "Really, donkeys?" She laughs a little too quickly, anxiously, and moves ahead.

"Stop!" Hooman instructs, walking on past her to a large salmon-pink metal gate.

The sound of Hooman's key scraping against the keyhole sends a surge of electricity from her toes to her chest.

He swings the gate open onto a vast slope of trees bearing hard tiny green balls.

To their right, narrow stairs lead to a balcony that hangs majestically over an orchard.

"Wow, amazing. What are those trees?" Leili asks breathlessly.

"Walnut trees. They fruit in the fall. Below them are fig trees. We'll take a walk down after we've rested."

He walks up the stairs to the balcony and opens the door to what was the caretaker's cabin. Leili pauses to look around before she follows him up the stairs.

"It's well hidden in the trees. I'd never have found it on my own."

"Welcome to my tree house," he says.

"Are you sure we'll be alone here?" She takes her shoes off at the doorway and enters the one-room cabin. The bare floor is cold beneath her feet.

"I'll lock the door."

"How did you get the keys?" Leili turns around to look at him.

"I had them made." He waits for her to disapprove and when she doesn't, he continues, "In the three weeks that I've been coming here no one has ever been by. I found this place one day when I was hiking. The gate was open and so I came in at sunset one evening and left at sunrise. The proprietor of the restaurant down the hill, Hajji, told me that the owner left during the Revolution. The government never reclaimed it. After two weeks of coming and going, I began to leave things here and finally had a locksmith put a new lock on the gate. I'm a squatter," he says, bowing his head in mock shame.

She wordlessly looks around the large empty room. There's a fireplace and a small tucked-away kitchen with a gas stove and a kerosene heater. A stack of lumpy mattresses leans tiredly against the wall. A single colorful tribal *gilim* covers the rotted wood floors. Faintly familiar smells of steamed rice, musty cushions, saffron and bergamot confuse her geographic sensors.

"It smells like my grandfather's house. Are you sure no one lives here?"

"Don't worry. Trust me, no one will come here this time of year. The bathroom is outside in the orchard and it's freezing."

She gives him a startled look.

"Exactly. Had I told you, you wouldn't have come."

"True," she laughs, making no move to remove her russari or rupush as she walks around to examine the cabin more closely. Hooman follows behind her and pulls her flowery scarf off her head, releasing a surprise of chestnut hair, which she pats down self-consciously.

"Hat hair," she says.

He hands her a pair of slippers.

"I'm going to make coffee. Will you start the fire? I know you're a bit of a pyromaniac—I've seen you burn through those candles." He squeezes her shoulder and walks past her into the kitchen.

"Wasn't me, I swear." Leili says smiling. She walks over to the fireplace and looks at the pile of fresh ashes below the unburned logs.

Hooman brings two cups of coffee and sets them down before her. He takes the matches that she hasn't touched and lights a fire.

They sit staring at the growing fire for a while, warming their hands and feet.

Finally, Leili says, "This place smells like my childhood painting teacher's studio."

"No paints here."

"Percolating espresso, musty pipe smoke and gurgling pigeons."

"Pigeons . . ." Hooman looks around as if he's missing something and says, "I hope not."

"The pigeons lived on the roof outside the little greenhouse my teacher built as his studio."

"Sounds ideal."

"Sometimes. He watched the Revolution from his balcony. He watched the city march below him in black and white, like ticker tape text that turned an Iran of many religions into an Iran of one religion."

"How dramatic. How so?" asks Hooman.

"He was also Armenian. I guess he never felt much at home after the Revolution."

"Is that how you feel?" Hooman asks.

"No. I wouldn't know the difference. My father was a Marxist— we only went to church to be with other Armenians. No, I'm more like the pigeons that stood watch with him—an observer without allegiances."

"A pigeon . . . interesting totem," Hooman jokes.

"His neighbors complained about the dirty pigeons. They gathered like a mass of outcasts on his roof and yet no one complained about his Saturday morning art students and we were as loud and messy as the pigeons: strutting around, gossiping and giggling."

"What patience the man had," Hooman says, laughing.

Leili chuckles when she recalls how loud and excited the younger students from the earlier class were when coming down the stairwell.

"The little girls giggled like crazy about the Picasso posters on his walls—not exactly how they imagined a naked woman's body," Leili says and blushes.

"Sounds like fun."

"It was. The rest of my life was so quiet. The silence at home, in my head, in all those damn engineering equations." Leili pauses to think how everything extraneous in her life was drowned out in his studio. "My neat life could be messy there." She stares into the fire and thinks how no one complained about paint spills on his bare concrete floors, or on the old yellowing walls. Easels, stools and paintbrushes littered the place, and yet the warm flood of light made it feel fresh, welcoming and safe. There were no drawn curtains or hidden agendas.

"And coffee?" Hooman points to her untouched cup.

Leili sips her coffee and says, "He brewed us coffee in a large French press, just like yours, and we sipped it daintily on the roof. We circled him like his gurgling pigeons to listen to him tell stories. He bought his apartment cheaply from a wealthy art collector who fled the country at the beginning of the Revolution. No one knows what happened to his art collection. It could still be hidden somewhere in that building."

Hooman's eyes twinkle. He packs tobacco into his pipe and says, "Go on."

"He had big glossy art books: German Expressionists, Klee, Nolde, and Kirschner. My teacher always smiled." Leili stops.

"But . . ." Hooman prompts her.

"He seemed sad." Leili shrugs her shoulders.

"Sad? His life sounds ideal."

"It was. I loved his studio. I wanted to move in! He just laughed at me and said, 'When, not if, but when you go to Paris, you must visit Maillol's studio. Then you'll see how an artist should live.' I couldn't imagine what he meant—his studio was heaven. He told me that I loved it only because I hadn't seen the possibilities the world has to offer. He tried to sound fatherly, but it came off a little depressed."

"What did the pigeons do while you were painting?" Hooman asks.

"They flew and explored. They were homing pigeons. At the end of our lesson he'd clap for their return. They flew home to him all at once from different directions and landed in a protective circle around his feet." Leili loved those last few minutes before she'd have to put her street covering back on, when she'd close her eyes and tilt her head back to face the sun. It was the only place her bare head felt the hot sun, where she could be so nakedly exposed.

"They cooed so gently." Every class she took deep breaths of the linseed oil used with the paints and the aroma of coffee, trying to preserve something she knew was fleeting. "Tehran is not a pigeon city," Leili concludes.

"I know what you mean," Hooman says.

"You do?" Leili takes a deep inhale of the sweet, sticky tobacco.

"Yeah, pigeons belong in a faraway city, a city of artists."

"But we are a city of artists. Why does it betray us, this city that we love?"

"Because we let it. Is this why you're scared to paint?"

"Scared?"

One day she pushed open the large wooden door to her teacher's lobby and only heard silence. Leili stares off into the orchard and imagines her teacher escaping in the half-light.

"What happened?" Hooman asks, coaxing her back to the present.

She sat down on the cold marble steps and waited.

"The apartment was locked. No sign of anyone but an old lady who dragged a shopping cart down the stairs . . ." It had never occurred to Leili that anyone else lived in the building but him.

"And?"

"She was a piece of work." Leili hisses to imitate the old lady. "Hsss . . . he should have told his students. Hsss . . . all week the same story. Hssss . . . this lobby is not a cemetery, go mourn somewhere else."

Hooman laughs.

"I asked her where he had gone. She looked at me with the satisfaction an old woman with emphysema might get at the misery of others."

"Schadenfreude," Hooman says. "Where'd he go?"

"Abroad. He won the lottery. A visa to the US." Leili can still see the sliver of light that came and went as the old lady passed through the doorway.

"I wanted to paint more than ever. I ran to the top of the stairs but the door to the roof was bolted shut. There was no note, no warning and no parting advice." Leili looks down at her hands where she has bitten her nails to the flesh. She continues, "I put my ear to the door and listened for cooing pigeons." She looks up at Hooman and asks, "How long do you think it will be before the pigeons fly off to a new home?"

"Maybe never. They may return there every night to look for him. Animals identify a person with a place."

"He left a few days before I met you."

In the garden snow turns to slush and crocuses peek through the wet soil. Hooman and Leili walk gingerly down the slope. When they reach the bottom Leili takes one long look at Hooman, turns and runs back up the hill to the cabin.

"I didn't know you were such a runner," Hooman pants as he reaches her at the top.

"Shhh . . . I hear something." Leili's heart thumps from the run and the sound of clinking and clanking outside the garden wall.

Hooman laughs. "It's a donkey bell. The farmer is heading toward the restaurants with fresh provisions. Come on, we need a few things."

Leili pulls her scarf out of her jacket pocket and ties it loosely around her head.

"Ali Agha," Hooman calls. "We need greens!"

The heavy bronze bell that hangs from the donkey's collar slowly stills. The animal stands motionless while his owner gathers bread, cheese, eggs and fresh greens from the two baskets hanging from his back. Leili gently pets the donkey's head and lightly touches the ceramic blue evil eye that hangs next to his bell.

"Your wife is here, may God bless her," the man says. He avoids Leili's eyes. "May God bless you with many children."

Leili blushes deeply and blurts, "Frozen Cokes?" She points to the crate of Coke bottles on the other side of the donkey's saddle.

"They are drinkable," the man says. Hooman takes a Coke and hands it to the man to open.

"We used to drink slushy Cokes on school ski trips to Dizin."

"Not so far from here," the man comments. "Lots of avalanches this year—the snow, then rain, then snow—the heavens are angry," he says as he leaves.

"You ski?" Hooman asks as they walk back into the garden.

"Not really. It was *the* thing to do in my high school. I hung out on the bunny hill—you know I'm terrified of heights. Once a friend made me go up on the lifts. When we were about to ski down I panicked and tried backing up. I ended up on the men's side of the rope. A Komiteh officer immediately showed up and yelled at me to get back on the right side of the line. I turned and fell right on top of him. My friend had a field day standing above him and quoting everything she could from the Quran about men touching unrelated women. I was laughing so hard, even though it was hard to breathe with this big man sprawled across me. He was so red and angry by the time he untangled me that he stomped off without even giving me a warning."

Hooman laughs. "You're an experienced woman."

"Hardly," Leili demurs.

The fire is dead when they return to the cabin. Hooman lights a kerosene lamp and sets up the corsi.

"Do you remember these from your childhood?" Hooman asks. He arranges the pillows around the low table and turns up the heat.

She shakes her head.

"Come sit. Put your legs underneath the table," he says. He throws a blanket over the table. "This is how poor provincials kept warm in the winters."

Hooman places a pillow behind her back. He catches her staring at him. "What is it?" he asks.

"I've never seen such long curly lashes on a man," she giggles.

"Sit tight, now you'll see a man make an omelet."

Hooman returns with a tray of hot bread, washed greens, and a beautiful omelet.

Leili takes the sheet of Barbari bread and rips it in half. "Someone's hungry," Hooman says smiling.

They spend the evening in front of the fire where Hooman has dragged a large box of books that he salvaged piecemeal from the bookstore before it closed.

"You read English, no? Take a look." He opens the box for her.

"They smell like my copy of *The Little Prince*."

"It's my pipe."

"Of course! You knew my book before I knew you. I thought the place seemed familiar . . . my father used to buy my books there, before . . ."

"Before?"

"He stopped leaving the house."

"How does he support you?"

"He has special permission to distill wine as an Armenian . . . for the church. He became his own best and only customer. Let's read this together." Leili pulls out a book of Hafez's poetry. They read to each other late into the night until Leili's eyelids feel like two heavy weights.

"You're not used to being up all night. Bedtime," Hooman announces.

Leili collects her towel and toothbrush and goes outside to the bathroom. It's cold, and she's anxious to be back inside where Hooman has set up a single mattress for her by the fire. He sits on another mattress a few feet away. She tries to hide her surprise.

"Take my quivering yellow weakness and give me your red-hot strength," he whispers to the fire as he watches her settle in next to it.

The fire is hot on her face. It burns her lips.

"Goodnight," she says and buries herself in her blankets; she thinks that she will never fall asleep with him so close, and so far.

When she's gently snoring, Hooman yawns and stretches. He quietly meditates a few feet away from her—close enough to feel the fire, far enough to protect the cocoon that he weaves slowly around himself.

Before he sleeps he walks past her bed to check the fire. He gingerly bends over and kisses her forehead before climbing into his own bed across the room.

Leili wakes in the night shivering. The fire has burned down. Moonlight illuminates the garden below.

She takes Hooman's coat and steps out into the cold and damp garden where the wet midnight dew gently settles on her shoulders. Underneath the fig trees in her flannel pajamas, bundled in Hooman's musky tobacco scent, she spies stars that pollution otherwise veils down in Tehran.

Leili walks into the dark room and observes Hooman's still form. She tiptoes to his mattress, lies down next to him and excavates for his warm heartbeat under layers of blanket. She cuddles up to his back and puts her arm around his shoulder. Leili holds Hooman tightly and pretends not to hear the rhythm of his alert eyelashes beat rapidly against his pillow.

In the morning Leili wakes alone. She stacks the mattresses and then steps out onto the balcony and watches Hooman move through the fig and walnut trees like a tall, thin wood sprite.

He returns with a bundle of warm fresh bread and a cold ripe fig that feels like velvet and tastes of the invigorating air.

They amble down the mountain, not quite ready to leave, to be separated. At the bridge Hooman takes Leili's hand and gently slides her ring off her finger.

"I know that you're a tiny bit superstitious," he says, "which is why we should ceremoniously throw this into the waterfall together."

"No!" Leili grabs for her ring. He pulls it away.

"You can't wear a ring that turns your finger green, and besides it's bad luck to buy yourself a ring." He continues softly, "Especially from a man who made dog tags for soldiers."

"What?"

He hands the ring back to her and says, "Go ahead and throw it."

"You're mad!" But she whips her right arm back and throws the ring as far as she can anyway. She looks back at him and says, "Pure tin."

He hands her a little box and says, "Open it." Inside is an octagonal-shaped yellow agate set in silver. The shiny stone surface is carved with a barely decipherable protective inscription. "It's the Hafez poem from the scrap of fortune you used to give me your phone number," Hooman says. "Green Seas and new moons. I hope that it will always protect you."

She slips the ring on and risks giving him a quick hug.

Dusk falls and strings of light illuminate the little cliff restaurants. Leili says, "My dad used to tell me that a fairy turned on the street lights when no one was looking. Sometimes we would wait together at the window to watch for the fairies to come. I believed so easily, so blindly just because someone I loved told me that they existed."

Hooman takes Leili's hand and says, "I believe in those fireflies you told me about, even though I've never seen them." She turns to leave him and as she does he brushes past the back of her covered head and says, "I should have kissed you."

She turns back to tell him that there will be other opportunities, but he is already gone.

بسم الله الرحمن الرحيم

In the Name of God

According to our teachers, the history of Iranian theater begins and ends with Ta'ziyeh, what a surprise! But we were definitely never taught about another little passion play. A little secret from the seventies is that one of the best theaters in Tehran was in Shahre-no, the red-light district. It was a large hall with simple, uncomfortable wood benches that no one sat on for long, even though the "play" could last all day and well into the night. No, the auditorium was more like a waiting room than a theater.

The red-light "actors" weren't great, but they had amazing stamina (in all aspects of their "art"). They had to, because at any given moment an actress might leave the stage without warning. The "company" ad-libbed a story—an unscripted soap opera that just kept going and going and going until an audience member winked at an actress, who would then exit stage left to see an "ailing grandmother" or "an old friend" or whatever fictitious plotline was awaiting her offstage. Then the man in the audience who had winked would also get up and leave. He wouldn't return, but the actress would—maybe half an hour, maybe an hour later, depending on her client's needs and the size of his wallet. When she returned to the stage, the other actors would ask after her ailing grandmother, her old friend, her own "health," which always got a laugh.

No wonder so many fathers freak out about their daughters becoming actors. I wonder if Leili has told her father? Some of the best actors in Iran were Armenian because Christians weren't as concerned with their daughters' piety! I read this in a book about Armenians. It's an old dog-eared thing I found. Was curious about Leili.

Blackout

"Movement is the ultimate meditation. When you move, twist, contort your bodies, it forces you to get out of your head and to stop thinking. See you next week," Hooman says.

As they pack up, Nima takes Arezoo's arm and touches the mess of green bruised skin that's only barely covered under a sweaty streak of caked-up beige makeup. "What's this?" he asks.

She pulls away and curtly says, "It's nothing. I'm first," she says and storms out barely dressed.

Nima makes a move to follow her. "Nima," Hooman reminds him.

Six months of practices and they continue to part like strangers: one by one they space their departures by a few minutes. During practice, there isn't time to talk and Hooman is obsessively careful and never allows anyone to linger near the theater afterwards.

When everyone else but Hooman has left, Leili turns and looks at the staircase. She absently counts the steps to the top.

"Hooman?"

She notices the quick, uneven staccato of her own breath. She inches back, just past the candle, where he can't see the expression on her face change.

"What's wrong?"

"I had this terrible dream and now I think I'm hearing things during practice," Leili whispers.

"Like what?"

"Doors opening, breathing . . . I don't know. It feels like someone is watching us."

"You're imagining things."

"Hooman, listen. I'm sure the door was unlocked when we came in," she whispers.

"You're nervous . . ."

"Maybe," she concedes and fades back into the dark.

Outside, the electricity is gone and everything is dark. Leili looks around for car lights to locate the main traffic square and spots a glow from the peephole. She stops cold, catches her breath and walks over to examine the light leak. Quickly, she places her bag over the hole to block the light and stands guard in the dark until Hooman appears, and then from the park—Kamran. They run into each other and pause a few feet away without seeing her.

"Where were you?" Hooman says.

"I've been right here," Kamran says. He gestures toward the general area. "Rehearsal's over."

Kamran lights a cigarette and waves it at Hooman.

"I quit," Hooman says and continues, "I don't care what you're up to on your own time, but if you want to be part of the performance, you come to rehearsal." He turns to walk away, changes his mind and instead asks, "Honestly, why do you bother?"

"You know the answer to that."

"Arezoo?"

"Please. When I met her, I actually wanted to try my hand at serious theater. Now I can see that it's not my calling."

"Why not split then. Why stay here and bother me?"

"You were an added bonus, guru," he laughs.

"I'm not trying to be anyone's guru."

"Oh really? You think you know everyone better than they

know themselves: marching around rehearsals, enlightening everyone with your inner knowledge; building silence around yourself like a moat. You have no idea who you are."

Hooman fumbles in his pocket for a cigarette. Leili waits to see if he'll find one, as he had ceremoniously handed her his "last cigarette" just before rehearsal.

Kamran lights another cigarette and hands it to Hooman, who ignores the offer.

"I'm warning you," Hooman says. "Show up or you're out."

Hooman turns to walk away. Leili runs after him.

"Hooman, wait."

He turns toward her, sheltering his cigarette from the wind.

"Are you OK?" she asks.

"Thanks," he smiles, smugly. "Everything's fine."

"And Kamran? He seems off," she notes.

"He's an actor . . . he's playing us."

"I'm not so sure. He's not a very good one." A small boy, a peddler, comes up behind Leili and she jumps.

Hooman throws him a coin. "You're a bundle of nerves. Why are you still here? You should be at home relaxing," he says.

"I waited to show you this. The electricity is out."

"So?"

"Come closer, look," she takes him to the peephole. "You can't tell now because the candle is out, but when you were still down there I could see the glow of your candle."

"Really?"

"How often do you think that we have been exposed like this?" asks Leili.

"In hundreds of hours of practice—who knows how often the electricity has gone out."

"Or how many casual pedestrians have seen the light," she says. "Didn't they stop rationing electricity after the war?"

Hooman doesn't answer. His head is bowed over the peephole.

"You look tired," Leili says.

He looks up at her and sighs. "I can't hold it all together."

"Hold what?" She looks up.

"Anything, everything." He looks out into the night.

"Who said you had to hold it all?"

"Who else will?"

"I thought you told us to release it."

"You're a quick learner. I want you to know that I hold your trust like a delicate bird in my palm." He pauses. "Now fly away home."

Leili turns hesitantly toward the dark traffic square and silent streets.

"Good-night," she says bravely.

"Want me to walk you? It's weird, this blackout."

"You're tired," she replies. "I'll go over to the taxi office and get a private cab." She turns swiftly toward a shortcut through the park before he can talk her out of it. She can just make out the safety of headlights in the distance and is almost to the sidewalk when a soldier emerges from the trees and intimately brushes past her.

"Ahhkkk," she protests. Goose bumps prickle her skin. She turns to tell him off but he stumbles and falls. He is drunk or high. She darts out into the middle of the street, flags down a taxi and pays for a private fare all the way home.

بسم الله الرحمن الرحيم

In the Name of God

They say that the main character should not only be flawed but that secondary characters should have a point of view. Is Iran the main character? Are we secondary characters ever allowed a point of view? Does anyone really know how to represent that point of view?

Writing manuals say bad things should happen to the protagonist. Well, that's easy. They also say the main character has her own spiritual quest and relationship with God and the universe. Is religion the main character? Religion is when the individual allows everyone else in bed with him/her and God. Religion is to talk publicly about a private spiritual relationship, inviting in rules, gatekeepers, experts, dictators of The Word . . . What kind of love affair is that?

I need a catchy title for the play. Nima wants to design flyers and I'm dragging my feet. Ideas:

Fireflies. Turns out their wings only keep them treading. They can't really fly—maybe not such a good title. I want my characters to fly.

Grounded. Like little kids who are not allowed to play? No, I want my characters to play and act out like naughty kids.

Acting out. But we're not naughty, not in God's eyes.

I'll call the play No Wings to Fly from God because not only are we completely grounded but we're stuck on earth with no escape from those who think they are doing God's bidding—a frightening prospect, really. What we want are some wings to fly to God, but that would be martyr-

dom and I'm not talking about such a physical flight, I'm thinking of a metaphoric one, a different kind of spiritual flight, one toward God rather than away from Him, because I'm pretty sure no one here is getting any closer to Him.

Leili keeps asking if the play is done. I still haven't given them the final scripts. They'll be doing a lot of ad-libbing while I'm doing a lot of fragment-like writing . . . like this:

> *He experiences her as if through the broken-mirrored walls of the Green Dome, in fragments of light and color, movement and memory. He weaves the threads of the play together during these conversations, during practice and while dreaming. He is no longer afraid to sleep, to dream . . .*

Friday
Leili tells me I only need to write dialogue. A written work should not just be a transcript, but an assault on the senses, on our ideas of what living is, on our entire moral and, if we're lucky, aesthetic code.

Maybe I'm trying to do too much? Leili says not to bother with stage directions . . . there's no stage.
Good point.

"I have nothing to lose."
"Neither do I."
"You don't believe that, otherwise you wouldn't be holding on so tightly."

I censor myself at every turn. It's gotten to the point where I no longer remember what's real and what's false. In the end is reality a mash-up? That's it. It's a play of fragments: bricolage. The scenes won't be in order: I'll hand a slip of paper to each audience member with a code and tell them to go home and rework the narrative from memory in order of the code to get the meaning.

Scene A:
A video projector shows footage of war propaganda (soldiers marching off to battle) against the backdrop of the city's propaganda (Leili's photographs of martyrs hang on the wall).
A soldier will be lying center stage—Nima or Kamran—dying. Arezoo will sing a mourning song. Leili will implore the audience to save him. This will continue until people are uncomfortable, until someone gets out of his or her seat and does something.
. . .
"And if they don't? What, do we just keep going?" Arezoo didn't like the idea much; she's afraid they won't have the stamina. I should tell her about the whores in the sixties who managed to act hours and hours at the red-light theater with extra "work" in-between scenes.

Leili will stay seated on the cold concrete stage and watch a light, a big fat spotlight, pass indiscriminately over her memory like time, like the ocean wearing down a piece of glass and softening the sharp edges until only a smooth, foggy exterior remains.

Honestly, I don't see anyone in the audience budging. I'll eventually have to stop the play. People are afraid of freedom, of choice, since it somehow denies God and makes everything meaningless, or as Dostoevsky says: permissible. There are few rebels in Iranian lore, just heroes and warmongers. Rebellion is a lonely concept in a follower society; the unveiled woman feigns madness to be free.

So, I gave Arezoo her stage directions: Scare them, taunt and tease them. Until every audience member is moved to save the soldier, we have work to do.

"You can't help people obtain freedom by forcing them into change," Arezoo said. She was taking me to her friend's place to listen to possible music for the play.

Arezoo doesn't see how fearless she is. How easy it is for her. She started unbuttoning her rupush the minute we entered the lobby of the apartment building. In the safety of the empty elevator she slowly *stretched her arms like a bird taking flight and released the long black robe that minutes ago had been so carefully buttoned at the nape of her neck. She unknotted her russari and let it fall from her head. She shook her full head of newly hennaed red hair, delighting in shedding her skin illicitly in the musak-filled cocoon, rising above the city to the theme song of* Love Story—*higher and higher above the accusing stares of the young martyrs who minutes earlier had peered down at us from city billboards and walls. We arrived at a plateau where morbid propaganda fades into a geography of beauty.*

Wall Flowers

The driver cranks his rust-colored Peykan into second gear while Hooman and Leili silently pray that it won't slip backwards as it putts its way higher and higher into the foothills of the mountains. In the rearview mirror, the city slips into black asphalt beneath their tires. The cabdriver is uncharacteristically quiet, and neither Hooman nor Leili attempt to make conversation.

The last of the day's light fades and the Alborz are miraculously visible in the unusually clean warm spring air that melts the mountain's snowy rupush to reveal tall craggy shoulders that tower over Tehran, nakedly, boldly, but not obscenely.

Hooman directs the driver to drop them off on the top of a vacant hill near an abandoned construction site.

"Where are we?" Leili asks, walking to the edge of the road.

"Kiarostami shot *Taste of Cherry* near here."

"That's the film where the man drives around interviewing people who will bury him after he commits suicide? Cheerful. You in the market for a gravedigger?" she jokes.

"No! And besides if you'd watched the extended version you'd see that he didn't go through with it. The sunsets here are amazing."

From above, in the orange and pink glow created by chemically combustible pollution, the city below looks like a plywood theater set, primed in black and ready for a set artist to paint the scene.

Glass mirrored panels on tall office towers shimmer in the dying light, sending out signals of incomprehensible code. Everywhere around them the dry brown world communicates something that they can't decipher. Below them gas lamps from the construction workers' makeshift shantytown glow like dying embers left by the sun. The Natural History Museum's dino statue a mile straight below them seems to roar in the dark prehistoric night.

They stop near the edge of a construction beam and silently watch the sky turn orange and red. "Your Valentine's Day card," Hooman says pointing to the pink sky.

"Three months and a country too late," Leili answers.

Hooman leads Leili down a truck path, past half-finished Persian palaces with Greek columns and Sassanian bas-reliefs perched high above the city, into a maze of villas and apartments scattered behind hedges and *baqalis*, makeshift grocers.

He stops in front of a two-story apartment building and rings the buzzer.

A young woman mummified in a shiny silver Lycra dress and peep-toe heels greets them at the apartment door.

"I'm a bit underdressed." Leili hesitantly hands the woman her rupush and russari, feeling naked in her flannel shirt and faded jeans.

"We're Arezoo's friends," Hooman explains.

"Want a drink?" the woman asks.

"Coke, please," Leili says. She looks around but finds it hard to see anything in the dim smoke-filled foyer. From the mounds of rupushes on wall hooks and on the bench it's obvious that there's a large party already in progress.

"And?" The woman waits.

"Tea?" Hooman says, even though the woman is still looking at Leili.

"Nothing with your Coke?" She waits.

"No, thanks."

The woman leads them down a long hallway, passing a number of people grouped in twos and threes, smoking what smells like an earthier incense than the ones at Leili's church.

"Arezoo's in the back room," the woman says pointing down the hall. "Drinks are in there." She veers them toward a large living room, adding, "Arezoo will be in soon."

"Should we go say hi?" Leili asks Hooman once they're deposited alone in the living room.

"No, she's probably warming up. Let's go get a drink."

"Warming up?"

"The band's playing a little concert," Hooman explains.

The salon is typical of most bourgeois salons in Tehran: Louis the XVI couches, Ionic columns . . . a long oakwood bar with glass cabinets and mirrors is built right into the wall at the end of the salon. Leili finds a single warm Coke next to a large plastic yogurt bucket of vodka. Next to it is an unopened Johnny Walker bottle and a mound of ice melting away in a silver bucket.

A waiter passes with a tray of tea.

"You didn't tell me it was one of these parties," Leili says.

"I didn't know. Last time it was a very hippie scene. People pay them to play at their parties." Hooman says.

They sit down with their drinks in the large empty circle of finely upholstered chairs.

"Where is everyone?" Leili asks.

"Back room," Hooman answers.

"Aha, the other guests." Hooman stands at mock attention when a crowd of tightly dressed and well-perfumed Tehranis waltzes in bearing more alcohol.

"I hid it under my chador," a minidress-clad woman whose hair is longer than her dress proclaims.

"God, I'm surprised the Komiteh didn't smell her coming," Hooman whispers to Leili.

"Shhh," Leili giggles. She stands to greet the new arrivals. Introductions are made. The lights are dimmed. A strobe light is turned on and a strong techno beat blares from three vibrating speakers within a few feet of each other.

"Live from LA!!" The crowd shouts "Yallah!"

Hooman chuckles but grabs Leili's hand anyway. "Get up—you wanted to dance."

He spins her around. "Where'd you learn to dance?" Leili shouts.

"What's there to learn? Just move!"

Leili moves her arms seductively, both parodying and enjoying the fusion of rock and Persian dance. Hooman grabs her, dips her, spins her and ever so briefly lifts her.

When the song ends they go to the kitchen in hopes of finding drinking water.

"Why aren't you performing with us?!" Leili shouts over the music.

"This is play—performing is different," Hooman says.

"What? You told me we were just playing, that you were teaching me to play," she says, looking around in a futile search for a hidden source of water.

"I take things too seriously . . ." Hooman gives her a smug smile.

She looks over at him and says, "You mean you're a perfectionist."

He shrugs and she goes back to her search for water. "The sink!" she announces, pointing to a faucet blocked and barricaded by boxes of booze and potato chips.

Arezoo runs into the kitchen, throws her arms around Hooman and shouts, "You came!"

He pulls back. "What the hell happened to your face?" he asks.

"Nothing."

"Where is he?"

"It wasn't him," Arezoo says. She looks Leili up and down and says, "You brought a guest."

"Hi," Leili says.

"I need to warm up," Arezoo says in response. She reaches past Leili and grabs a bottle of vodka. "Later," she says and leaves. Leili stares after her.

"Let's go catch our breath out on the balcony," Hooman suggests. He gently places his hand on Leili's lower back and steers her through the mess of caterers bringing in the dinner dishes.

Fans buzz at full speed, blowing the scent of food, alcohol and perfume through every corner of the hot and crowded salon.

"*Fesenjoon!*" Leili exclaims, "My favorite!" The smell of the walnut and pomegranate sauce overpowers the other dishes as the waiters walk in with trays piled high with basmati rice and stews like *Ghormeh sabzi* and fesenjoon. Next come mounds of lamb kabobs and chicken kabobs marinated with sumac, butter and lime which are placed next to a large antique ceramic bowl decorated with the Zoroastrian sun god and filled with a salad of fresh lettuce covered in a confetti of shredded beets and carrots. Silver dishes filled with thick, creamy yoghurt with shallots are scattered across the table, along with various pickles (eggplant, cauliflower, cucumber and carrot). Plates of fresh herbs (mint, basil and chives) and hot flatbread top off the buffet.

"We should get in line now," Leili insists. Every Iranian party has a mad dash to the buffet, when people who earlier fell over themselves to be polite will elbow and push each other to get to the endless food.

"I'm thinking I might go straight for desert," Hooman says, pointing to the table's centerpiece, a crème caramel molded like a swan and drizzled with honey.

"What we really need are one of these." Leili takes two glasses filled three-quarters full with a thick green melon shake and hands one to Hooman.

"We need air more than food," he says, pointing to the balcony door.

Just as they reach the door, a man in tight black jeans and a Red Hot Chili Peppers shirt stops Hooman and gives him a quick hug and pat on the back. Hooman says hello in passing and follows Leili outside. He shuts the door securely behind them.

"Mmmm," Leili says, facing the cool, calm air. "How did you know that guy?"

"Which guy?"

"The hipster."

"The *khanegah*, oddly. He's also an Arezoo-ex."

"He's hardly the Sufi type."

"Guys with problems—love, drugs, alcohol, depression—think that time in a Sufi lodge will cure them."

"Does it?"

"Not really. Not if they don't believe. Sufism is the relinquishing of ego and these guys are holding onto theirs for dear life. They can't see how it's the cause of all their problems in the first place."

"Is that why you went?" Leili asks carefully.

"No. My uncle was a Sufi. He lived and worked in the khanegah in Mashhad. His life's work was to lovingly and humbly replace broken tiles in a centuries-old lodge—The Green Dome. When the bookstore closed and I had nowhere to go I called on his brothers in Tehran . . . that's where I took you. I slept there for some nights before moving to Nima's and then the orchard. They loved my uncle. They'd do anything for him."

"Is he still . . ."

"Listen," Hooman cuts her off abruptly. "Sounds like a patrol car in the street."

Hooman crouches down and carefully goes to the edge of the balcony and peers over.

"Shit, Komiteh. They have paddy wagons."

"What?"

"Don't panic. Follow me." Hooman grabs Leili's hand tightly and pulls her to the ground. He inches toward the railing of the balcony.

"I'm scared," Leili whispers. She crawls with him to the edge of the balcony and slumps down against the railing.

"It's not as high as it looks. We do this in practice all the time. I'll climb down and break your fall . . . but you won't fall, I'm sure. You can climb down it."

"Climb down it?" Leili shrieks.

"A broken arm is better than a night or more in prison . . ."

"Hooman," tears well in Leili's eyes.

"You can do it."

"I'll hide here," Leili insists.

"Where? There's no cover and this is the first place they'll look. Promise you'll follow? I need to go first to catch you." The music and lights go off in the living room.

"They're coming. Please Leili, trust me." Hooman moves toward the edge of the balcony. "They'll be up here in a minute. We have to wait until they leave the street and enter the stairwell and then jump down before they make it to the apartment door. Follow my lead."

Hooman takes a deep breath and slips over the side of the wall with the ease of a scuba diver falling off the edge of a ship. Leili peers over the balcony and immediately backs away. She hears a crash just inside the balcony door. A light goes on in the living room. She darts over to the balcony and pulls herself over the ledge; just as she does a gruff male voice yells, "Over there, the balcony, on the wall."

Without looking, she lets go and falls. Hooman catches her and tumbles with her into the driveway. He jumps to his feet, grabs her hand and they run as fast as they can toward the hills until it's too dark to see or be seen. When they can no longer hear frantic voices and the slamming of metal paddy-wagon doors—the general panic and frenzy of the police bust—they fall down panting.

"What happened to climbing down the wall?" Hooman laughs.

"I was nervous. Are you OK?" Leili asks, "Sorry, I fell pretty hard on you."

"I'm fine. What about you?"

"Just a scrape," Leili says, rubbing her thigh. "Arezoo's crazy. That party was riskier then what we're doing in the theater."

"Take my flannel shirt and hat. You're naked out here without a rupush and russari."

"Damn." Leili winds her hair up expertly and stuffs it into his hat.

Hooman smiles. "Now who's the Basij?" He takes her chin and turns it, pretending to study her new look. "All you need is a beard," he says and pulls her face to his. He pauses to catch his breath and then he kisses her.

"Sorry, it's the adrenaline." He lets go of her chin.

"Amazing stuff," Leili says breathlessly. She looks behind her. "We're alone."

"That could change," he says and wraps her in his shirt.

"I'm hungry."

"Those Komiteh are likely all over the dinner we were never served," Hooman says.

"I'm scared for Arezoo. We're not in high school anymore. These guys aren't as easily bribed; they actually believe in what they're doing."

"I know," Hooman says solemnly.

Leili thinks for a minute. "Pizza?"

Hooman laughs. "Where?"

"Tajrish? It's Thursday night and Tajrish is hopping; we could pick it up and take it to your place. I'm supposed to be spending the night at a friend's." She bites her lip and smiles at him.

"Oh really?" Hooman, emboldened by the privacy of the vacant dark night, kisses her again.

By the time they reach the door to his garden, the pizza they've carried up the mountain is cold and soggy and quickly forgotten for more appetizing, exciting and novel nourishment.

Hooman begins by reclaiming his shirt but doesn't stop until Leili's in her bra and panties.

"Let's examine that scrape," he says.

Leili giggles.

"Where is it?" he asks.

She points to her thigh.

He leans over and brushes a gentle kiss on her thigh. "Soft," he comments.

"Here too," Leili points to her other thigh.

Hooman takes it in his hand and rubs it. "Muscular," he says. "Where else?"

"Hard to say, it was a long fall," she whispers.

Hooman leans over, and beginning with her toes, examines her entire body with little kisses.

"Is this the first . . . ," Hooman starts.

"Shhh . . . ," Leili says.

At her waist he puts a finger beneath the elastic of her underpants and asks softly, "Permission?"

"Granted," she whispers.

بسم الله الرحمن الرحيم
In the Name of God

They stand in tree pose, reaching for the unseen sky above them. Their collective breath comes to life like a jump-started car that is at first shallow and fast, then deep and smooth.

I can't write what I'm feeling . . . I can't concentrate.

Shadows

Leili reaches up beyond the unseen sidewalk where students rush home to dinner, where the eight o'clock theater audience is already lined up outside the ticket box, where the Komiteh lie in wait and where junkies pace, their needles dropping through the peephole.

"Deeper," Hooman whispers. "Arms up above your heads—on your toes, stretch, stretch." Hooman reaches up above his head and stretches toward the ceiling—perfectly balanced. Leili peeks at him and loses her balance.

"Look straight ahead and focus inward. You lose your balance watching others," he admonishes her gently.

Leili's body is a pendulum that sways to and fro in the dark.

"Is Arezoo OK?" Leili asks Hooman once the others have safely left. "Did anything happen? I didn't want to ask . . . she looks a little worn-out."

"She wasn't there when the police came," Hooman says.

"But we saw her."

"Apparently she fought with her boyfriend and took off with the vodka."

"Wow, that was lucky."

"Yeah," Hooman whispers.

"I'm . . . ," Leili starts to say. The candle outlines Hooman's freshly shaven jawline.

"I'm not used to you clean-shaven."

He doesn't answer. His long black lashes throw shadows beneath his eyes.

"You look tired," she says.

He touches her face and traces the dark shadows that circle her eyes like curled-up earthworms. "You too."

He glances at his hands and the candle that has burned down to his fingertips. Another candle collapses nearby. Darkness is imminent.

"Leili . . ." He kisses her gently. "I want to stay here with you, but we should . . ." He hesitates.

"I know. It's time to go," she says. "Meet later?"

"I need to attend to something tonight," he says carefully. "Tomorrow?"

She gathers her things and mutely makes her way up the stairs. She pauses halfway and looks back. She can just make out Hooman's cross-legged shadow sitting in the dying light.

He takes a small book and rubs his fingers along its outer edge. The book's shadow is bumpy and Leili imagines how the deckle page-edge of a water-damaged book must feel like the edge of a smooth but uneven shell. He opens it to a random page. Hafez, she guesses, divination. He mutters something like a mantra. He told her that he had stopped practicing religion when he was a young boy, but tonight it almost sounds as though he's begging the dark for guidance.

The Graveyard Shift

Little drops of rain on the windshield grow larger and larger as they drive toward what Leili guesses is a shortcut to Darband. But just before the Darband Road, the taxi turns into a little villagelike neighborhood of Chizar and stops in front of the green gates of an Imamzadeh—the final resting place of a Muslim saint.

When Leili was a child her nanny often took her to an Imamzadeh and taught her how to gently kiss the gold cage and tie a ribbon on one of its bars in exchange for a miracle. It was a ritual that oddly calmed her in a way that going to church never does. She always felt the presence of angels in the Imamzadeh–she hasn't felt or thought about those visits in years. She wonders if Hooman's ribbon is already hanging from the cage and what miracle he might need badly enough to come here in the middle of the night.

"You kids are sly. The Komiteh would never look for couples here," comments the cabbie. Leili isn't listening.

"Here you are," he says, louder this time. When she doesn't move, he asks, "Are you getting out?"

"Are you sure this is where the other taxi came?" she asks meekly. She waited for Hooman to leave the theater and followed him across the street.

"Yes, I am sure." He looks at her through the rearview mirror and asks, "Shall I wait for you? Do you have a date or don't you?" he asks.

"No," Leili says haughtily.

"He went in there." He points to the cemetery that surrounds the Imamzadeh. He doesn't offer again to wait for her.

She pays him and steps out into the pouring rain and squints at the wet green metal gates to the cemetery. A man turns the corner under a lamp. He is bent over with age but wears a blue wool cap like Hooman's and so she follows him through dark heavy rain toward the Imamzadeh. Is he going to make a wish? He turns toward her and she ducks behind one of the few trees and watches him walk deeper into a forest of gravestones. Her palms sweat. She wants to run after him, but is afraid of what she might discover—in the cemetery in the dark.

The figure turns another corner, and Leili has to come out of the shadows and into the open to follow him into what looks like a garden that surrounds the little shrine. She wishes that she had a chador.

The rain has covered any hints of recent mourning activity like freshly watered flowers, upturned dirt, a washed gravestone or a new portrait . . . Christians don't use pictures on gravestones. But here, all that's visible is a harvest of dead faces—young and old faces, in plain clothes and military fatigues. Startled, she steps back and looks away but there's nowhere to avert her gaze where a dead boy does not watch her. She stands among them, alive, female, an anomaly among the black-and-white photo portraits placed between two pieces of glass like slides on a microscope.

Not one of the dead faces gives her a welcoming smile. They cannot speak to admonish her for not wearing a chador or to comfort her because she is soaking wet. Why so many men? She looks around and realizes that even though this is northern Tehran and a saint's tomb, she is standing in the center of a cemetery populated by martyrs.

She steps back, burned by the realization. A few rows ahead of her, the bent figure kneels before the grave of a young martyr. She gasps. The man turns toward her—his face is old and knotted

with muscles that no longer move, pinned into place by splintering, arthritic bones.

"The cemetery is closed," the old man tells her. She barely hears
him under the rain.

"I thought you were someone else. I'm looking for my cousin.
Maybe you saw him?"

The man sits back on his heels and studies her carefully.

"I haven't seen him in a long time," he says.

"Was he here? Has he already left?" she asks.

"What I meant was that he hasn't been here in the cemetery
before tonight—not for a long time." He looks at her, thoughtfully.

"You haven't been to a martyr's cemetery before." He pauses
and takes another look. "No, no. Not the type."

She doesn't respond.

"So you're the reason that he no longer comes here, the reason
for his agitation tonight, the one who caused him to rush here in
the middle of the night in the pouring rain."

"You know him?"

"Not really, but my loyalty lies with his kind," the man answers.

"When did he leave?" Leili yells over the rain.

"Maybe half an hour ago. I have been here so long that one
minute feels like the next."

"Was it raining when he left?" Leili asks.

"It may just have been." The old man answers thoughtfully.
He turns away from her and bends over to brush dirt off of a
grave. He caresses the indentations in the stone where letters
carve out the name of a dead boy.

Leili wipes the rain out of her eyes and looks around.

"It's over there." The man points to a grave with fresh flowers.

Leili goes to the grave and looks at the picture. It's as if a teenage Hooman stares back at her. The tombstone claims he was
born in Mashhad and died twelve years ago, at the front, on this
very night.

بسم الله الرحمن الرحيم
In the Name of God

I want to light up the stage. Set it on fire. And then I want to jump into it like a moth to the flame . . . rapture. Rupture? Why is death at the core of love? Why must it invade every romantic moment?

Soldiers

One by one, they step into the candlelight to show Hooman their backbends, lifts and leaps—their bodies then form into a single mass that moves through silence.

The warm egg-colored light outlines their forms like weakly drawn watercolors—brown and pink, yellow and olive.

"Imagine music. Feel it tap faster than your own heartbeat."

Leili bends toward Hooman's voice.

"Notes should fly off of your bodies and crash into the audience like out-of-control cymbals," Hooman says from the shadows.

Arezoo moves into the space that the light has left warm in its wake and spins like a dervish, carefully and in control. One hand reaches for heaven, the other for the earth.

Hooman directs her as if she were a marionette with invisible strings to lean over Nima, who rolls under her into a perfect tumble and lands at Leili's feet.

"Don't touch her!" Hooman corrects him.

"I'm not."

Nima does a headstand that Leili gently arches back against. Her long fingertips reach back for the last of the light. She bends from the waist until her face is washed in light. The light is always brightest as it dies.

Their grunts and stomps, their sheer energy is deafening even in its silence. Any noise that does escape is safely covered by a crash of thunder from outside.

"We are communicating with Jupiter," says Hooman.

Spring rain cracks and crashes into the pavement and the world thaws overhead.

"We're done moving in chains—time to learn to fly," he says.

Arezoo cackles, "Then why the hell are we on stage in bandages?"

"It is a bit difficult to move," Nima agrees.

"Paralysis, metamorphosis . . . you must move out of your bandages like a . . ." Hooman pauses. "Like a . . ." he tries again.

"Like a moth from a cocoon." Leili finishes his sentence.

"A moth is attracted to light but if it gets too close—if it embraces the light, the light consumes it," he says.

"Rumi," Leili whispers.

"Not all desire is mystical," Nima mutters.

"Not all moths are attracted to flame," Leili shoots back at him. She looks for Hooman's outline in the dark.

"Not all flame is strong enough to kill a moth," Arezoo says. She glances dramatically at their dying candle. "Some moths get burned without dying. Now, can we please move on? I don't want to be down here for hours again like yesterday." Her voice is cranky and tired. "What's the premise, Hooman?"

"Visualize this space as a bomb shelter."

"Why would we *ever* want to do that?" Arezoo stops and asks.

"It's an exercise," Hooman replies. Over the past couple of weeks he has introduced acting exercises where they imagine themselves walking among rows of naked bodies, standing knee-deep in mud. Tonight he chooses a scenario closer to home and asks them to "imagine war."

"War?" Nima stops in protest.

"Just for improvisations. Don't worry, keep going," Hooman says.

"War?" Leili asks.

"I want to use my voice," Arezoo reminds him.

"Soon," Hooman assures her.

"Where is Kamran, anyway?" asks Arezoo.

"It smells in here," Nima says, scrunching his nose.

Hooman ignores him and says, "Come on, go. Imagine bombs flying at you out of nowhere—a mile a minute from the dark." His voice chases Leili.

"When the audience is seated we will blow out the candles and begin in absolute darkness." Hooman's voice is low and emphatic.

Nima blows out the candles. Darkness enfolds them. They fall still for a moment while their inner compasses spin for direction.

"Wow," Leili says softly under her breath.

"It's like opening your eyes on a patch of black velvet," says Arezoo.

"It's as if my pupils are taking a bath." Leili squints into the darkness.

"Are you imagining the bombs coming at you? Move," he directs them.

Arezoo tiptoes across the room.

"I can almost see them." Leili pretends to duck from a missile. "It's hard to imagine light in the dark," she says out of breath.

"It's not a wash, or a flood of light, but a spark," he tells them. We'll use flashlights in the actual performance. We'll also have a video backdrop which will lend some light."

Nima marches past them straight-legged and at attention.

Leili's fingertips gently graze the cold cement wall and a shock shoots through her. "Something's wrong," she whispers.

"Good," says Hooman, "that's the right impulse."

"But, I . . . ," she says, suddenly afraid.

"How does it make you feel?" Hooman's voice is bigger in the dark.

"Like I'm in a grave, buried." Leili is the only one to answer.

"A grave?"

Following him the other night into the cemetery has scared her, made her less sure of the world—of him. She stops running, ignores the imaginary bombs and carefully avoids the walls. They've all memorized this path; there is no need for light.

"Okay," Hooman says, "That's good for now."

Nima strikes a match and a muffled scream burns through the dark.

Leili falls to the ground and covers her head.

Hooman laughs, "Excellent improv, but no screaming."

"I didn't scream," says Leili.

They stand frozen in the dark, listening for the sound that Leili never made.

In a dark corner Arezoo holds her mouth with one hand and the wall with the other.

"Arezoo, come on, not yet . . . ," Hooman starts but stops when he follows her gaze to the dirty ground where a combat boot sticks out from beneath a gunnysack.

"It's just a boot, kick it away," he tells her.

"It's heavy—I almost tripped over it, I think it's connected to some . . . ," she gags, "thing . . . ," Arezoo whimpers.

Hooman gently tries to lift the combat boot. He tugs at it but can't lift it. Arezoo bends over and pulls at the corner of the gunnysack. Leili screams and Arezoo drops the material before she's fully pulled it off the body's face. It's a man in military fatigues.

"He isn't moving," Leili mutters.

"He's dead," Nima says without checking. "It smells."

Hooman stares at the body wordlessly, covering his mouth with his hand as though he might get sick.

"Hooman?" Leili cries out.

Nima moves slowly and silently over to their pile of clothes as if he might wake the dead man or suddenly attract attention. They remain as silent as the dead soldier save for Arezoo, who is desperately trying to control herself, which only makes her sobbing that much louder. Maybe it's better than sudden silence, thinks Leili as Nima hands her a rupush and russari in a strange slow motion. Without checking whether they're hers, she puts them on and turns to Arezoo, whom Nima is gently covering with a rupush.

"Hooman, you of all people cannot be here if we're caught. Go," Nima warns him.

"Hooman?" Leili implores. His face is vacant, transformed—absent.

"Leili come," Nima says as he slowly leads Arezoo away from the half-covered dead body that lies in the corner of their theater. She clings to him while he quickly gathers their things. With their backpacks over one shoulder and Arezoo holding the other, Nima starts silently up the stairs.

Leili turns away from the body. "Hooman?" Leili whispers, waiting.

"Go. Carefully. Get out."

"Come?"

"Yeah." Hooman backs away from the body. "I'm not sure . . ." tears well up in his eyes.

Leili turns toward him. She puts her hand on his shoulder. "Come," she repeats.

"Oh my God," Hooman mutters.

"Not here," Leili whispers urgently. "Come."

He grabs her and holds her tight. "Please Hooman, let's get out of here."

At the top of the stairs he tells Leili to go first.

"Leili," Nima calls to her from the brightly lit fountain. He holds Arezoo's shoulders while she leans over and retches into the fountain.

"Where's Hooman?" he asks.

"Should we call an ambulance?" Leili asks hoarsely.

"Shhh . . . ," Nima says, "the police."

"It's too late. He's dead," Arezoo says between heaves.

"Someone must've seen us come out of there just now. We have to tell the police. We have no choice," says Leili.

"No!" Arezoo bolts upright. "Where's Hooman?" she demands weakly.

They look around and notice that he's disappeared.

Arezoo drops her head between her legs. Leili takes a bottle of water from her knapsack and helps Arezoo take a drink.

Leili says, "Hooman's probably gone to find Mashti. To warn him."

"Shit," Arezoo says, "We should leave."

"We should wait for him," Leili protests.

Arezoo puts her hand to her forehead and sways. Nima steadies her.

"Leili, help me get Arezoo home," Nima says.

"No," she stammers and as if suddenly remembering an important piece of information, asks, "Where's Kamran?"

"Shhh." You're going to get us arrested. "Who cares about Kamran?"

"Find him, please," Arezoo begs. Leili and Nima exchange glances.

"Sure," Nima says, taking Arezoo's hand. "Come on."

Leili and Nima walk Arezoo two blocks down Vali Asr to a private taxi company. A bell sounds as they open the door into the small waiting room awash in neon. A tired-looking dispatcher revived by the bell looks up at them as they walk in.

"The light hurts," Arezoo says. They help her into one of the two chairs.

Nima gives the dispatcher his home address.

"My mom will take care of her," Nima says to Leili as they

walk outside. "She needs a sleeping pill, and my mom is a walk-ing pharmacy."

"Who was it?" Leili whispers.

"The body?" Nima asks.

Leili nods her head.

"He was in a soldier's uniform. He overdosed."

"How do you know?"

"This place is crawling with druggies," he says, reminding Leili of the other night. She says, "Oh, God . . . there was a soldier in the bushes. He must have been high." Leili feels queasy.

"Go inside," Nima says.

"It's a bad omen" Leili mutters under her breath.

Nima frowns. "It's hardly an omen if the bad thing has already happened." He turns his face away from approaching headlights.

"Go, that's your car," Nima says.

"Where are you going?" She asks him.

"To wait for Hooman and Mashti." He turns around and walks away.

Leili walks back inside the taxi office. Arezoo looks greener under the neon lights. Leili sits down beside her. "You OK?"

Arezoo looks up at Leili and asks, "Has Hooman come back?"

"No," Leili says softly. She places a hand on Arezoo's shoulder.

"He'll be back," Leili says tentatively.

"And Kamran. We have to find him," Arezoo says.

The man looks up, obviously eavesdropping. He says, "Your friend was here."

"Friend?" Arezoo asks the man.

"You folks have been in before. He's dropped you off for a cab," he says pointing at Leili.

"Was he wearing a hat?"

"Blue wool cap?" The man asks.

"Yes," Leili says.

"The driver took him north, to Darband."

Arezoo looks at Leili and says, "Take the taxi. Go get Hooman. I think you know where to find him. No?"

Leili ignores the implication and says, "Later. We need to get you home first."

"There isn't any time for that. I'll be OK until the next taxi comes. Go," Arezoo insists while mustering all the energy she can to wave Leili toward the door.

Leili hesitates. Sweat streaks Arezoo's heavy makeup and exposes dark bruises of sleeplessness under her eyes. It somehow produces the unexpected effect of making her look much younger, like a little girl. She waves Leili off. "Go. If you don't, I will."

Leili runs out to the taxi, opens the passenger door, sticks her head in and looks earnestly at the taxi driver. "I'm looking for my cousin. He had on a blue wool cap," she says breathlessly.

The cabby says, "Get in." He looks at his watch and says, "It's late. Past curfew."

He puts the car in gear and turns toward the mountains.

In the rearview mirror Leili sees Arezoo slip out of the taxi stand and into the night.

Residue

"It's OK, it's OK," Leili says.

Hooman opens his eyes briefly, then turns over and falls back asleep.

Leili returns to the little kitchen where the light of the samovar's gas burner glows orange and blue through the night. The cabin is warm and quiet and smells of saffron and bergamot. A kitten gently meows on the balcony. Leili suspects that Hooman feeds it and so she takes a small bowl of fluffy white rice and coaxes the kitten to the door. She gently runs her finger over her small soft, dirty gray spine. The familiar smell of diesel and wet concrete that's stuck to her body from the city below could almost convince her that nothing outside has changed in the past five hours since they found the soldier. Up here in the orchard, shadows form dragons and her heart still flutters slightly at childhood fears that wait for her in the dark. Leili pours a cup of tea, knowing it's a bad idea to mix caffeine and insomnia.

"Leili?"

Hooman lies on his side in a fetal position. He looks like skeletal remains. Sweat soaks through his T-shirt and leaves impressions of his movements on his sheets—a streak marks his shoulder blade, a faint line draws a circle around the indentation of his thin waist.

"What was that noise?" he whispers.

"You had a nightmare," Leili says softly.

Hooman rolls over and turns his back to her. He takes a long, deep breath, inhaling the smell of damp earth and spring rain. In a soft, lucid voice, he says, "You're here."

"I didn't want to wake you."

He sits up and hugs her tightly. When he lets go he says, "I wish last night were a nightmare that I could wake from."

"Is that what you were dreaming about?"

"I was dreaming that I was in a hospital during the war. That's all I remember."

Hooman leans back against the wall. He feels around for a pack of cigarettes.

Leili inches closer. She sits alongside him quietly. His hands shake as he lights his cigarette. "It smells like the marshes in here," he says.

"They're hundreds of miles away."

Hooman stares out the open window into the comforting and familiar dark.

"I want to write." He points to his journal on the table next to her. She hands it to him. "Can you write for me?" He hands it back to her with a pen. "Write: The marsh crawled over them like a silent monster—wet, cold and frightening. It settled them deep into the crevices of the empty night and hid them from the enemy, from each other and eventually from themselves."

"Who, Hooman?"

"The soldiers."

"It was just a dream, a residue. That's all dreams are—residue."

Hooman nods. He drops his cigarette ashes into the palm of his hand. Leili looks around for an ashtray.

A Muezzin taps the microphone in a faraway mosque and clears his throat before he announces the dawn prayer. Hooman darts up to slam the window shut.

"What happened, Hooman?" Leili asks hesitantly.

"Gauzy layers of bandaging cover me like a mummy and I'm not sure if I'm dead yet. I can't remember how to move. I'm in the marshes of the Shat Al Arab and a bullet grazes right past me, offering me a fast track to paradise—but I refuse. My chin is raised at the sky as I fall."

"Is this the play you're writing?" Leili asks softly.

Hooman shakes his head and continues, "The worst part of the dream isn't even in the marshes but in the hospital trailing the bobbing light of the nurse's lantern. The light teases and taunts and shoots far away from me. I can see it but can't catch it. It moves through the dark hall like insects on fire. I remember now, even the insects burned and fell to the earth like little meteors." Hooman clears his throat and looks out the window.

"Like our rehearsal last night."

"Maybe."

"You screamed for candles. You were dreaming about our theater," Leili coaxes softly.

"No, it's a recurring dream I have about the war and of a nurse's face that I can't see. I lost my own face, my feet, my hands, myself—in the dark."

"Are you sure the dream wasn't about last night? There was a soldier . . . Do you remember?" Leili asks.

"I wanted to go back . . . I went to alert Mashti, then it got so late."

Leili thinks of Arezoo slipping away, but doesn't say anything.

"What happened?" Hooman asks.

"Who was he?"

"The soldier?"

"The one you knew. The one you went looking for in the rain."

Hooman studies her carefully, not sure he heard her correctly.

"I followed you last week," Leili admits.

"My father and my brother both died in the war . . . at the front."

Leili looks down at her hands. "I saw. Your brother . . . his grave."

"He volunteered," Hooman's voice trembles.

"Willingly?" She moves closer to him.

"I was in elementary school when they left. My brother was fourteen. He died at fifteen." He looks out into the dying light. "Kidnapped, really . . ." He clears his throat and says, "My neighborhood was not a wealthy one; Mashhad is a religious city. All of my neighbors were religious. All anyone talked about was the front. They showed films about martyrdom on TV, the mosque, at school. My brother wanted to play with guns, to be a hero, and so when my dad was drafted, he went along." Hooman's voice wavers. He looks at Leili to see that she's following before continuing, "My grandfather was illiterate, but he took my religious education upon himself. What a preacher—what a turn-off. My mother spent every minute after the war ended looking after me and searching for my brother and dad. We spent weeks traveling to the former front and attending returned POW parades. I slept in barracks and in ditches, waded in marshes hoping not to stumble on a mine, which many did. God, the front was awful. And you couldn't just visit; you had to go through the whole damn melodrama—the reenactments, the speeches."

"No wonder you're so good at theater."

"Civilians had no idea what the front was like. Iran was always short of soldiers. I don't know how we lasted eight years. We should have lost in the first six months." Hooman pauses to examine Leili's reaction.

"I don't understand. Why didn't your dad or brother leave?"

"They shot deserters. No matter what anyone tells you, we lost the war."

"I know," Leili says, gently.

"They never saw the enemy, but Saddam saw them. Like your fireflies. They couldn't kill their light—there was still nowhere they could hide where they would not be found. He had radar. As soon as you were seen you were dead." He pauses, rubs his eyes and sits up straighter.

"Your poor mom."

"My mother only gave up looking for my dad when she went crazy, literally. The Martyrdom Foundation Goodwill Charity paid to institutionalize her. How's that for irony?" He looks up at Leili. "Now the battlefield is daily life."

"What do you mean?"

"The soldier last night had needle marks all up and down his arm." He looks out the window, thinking.

"Kamran has disappeared," Leili tells him.

"And Nima?"

"He was waiting for you and Mashti when I left," she answers.

"And . . . ," Leili begins to say.

"And?" He prods her.

"Arezoo took off . . . back toward the theater."

بسم الله الرحمن الرحيم

In the Name of God

Leili is sitting here, watching me—forcing me to write. She thinks it's good therapy. At least it gets me out of making dinner.

The more I try to write, the more the ideas escape. Meaning doesn't find a place to sit still but bounces off the walls, and when caught, I regard it as a caged bird and release it. I need to hold onto something. And what keeps coming back to me? The war. The f-ing weight of history is crushing creativity.

Leili told me about her recurring dream where the sky was lit up with fireflies. She was abroad, in one of those pink- or baby-blue-colored countries in encyclopedia maps where fireflies come from. She tried to catch the fireflies with the other kids, and when she finally caught one it exploded in her hand. Her dream stopped when she met me.

Mine hasn't. It's always the same damn dream: I'm staring at a wall waiting for the light of a bomb to illuminate an escape route. But I blink every time and miss my out.

Tendrils of wet marsh reeds wind around me—to bandage me or to drown me? They prick holes in my skin where my soul slowly leaks out.

I miss my dad, even though I don't really remember him anymore. He spent a year at the front, separated from my brother, who was in the marshes, barely hidden by the long sharp reeds. He lived in a gunboat— they were wet all the time. Mushrooms grew out of their sneakers. They were given metal daggers that looked like kebab skewers to wave at the enemy. The swords were from the sixth century—probably looted from a museum, too dull to do any harm. He wrote to us that he thanked God that he never actually had to defend himself with one. He said that the war was torture and there wasn't a single day he didn't want to die. He had lost his faith completely. A fellow soldier friend of my brother's visited us in Mashhad and told my mom that martyrdom became suicide. He said, "Thousands of boys stormed the enemy, not to die in the line of battle and enter God's paradise, but to save themselves from the terror of gas attacks, chemical weapons, starvation. The world thinks that they stupidly stormed the front line with their bodies for spiritual salvation, but it was suicide." His voice cracked; he was still young when he came to recount to us the horror of what he'd seen. Sometimes security, fighting for our country, what we think of as a safety measure is a worse form of violence.

Leili's asleep. She told her parents she's with a sick friend. I can't sleep . . . I'm translating. It takes my mind off of things. Agha Jerzy says, "Private conflicts, quarrels, sentiments, animosities are unavoidable in any human group. It is our duty towards creation to keep them in check insofar as they might deform and wreck the work process. We are obliged to open ourselves up even towards an enemy."

This enemy must be faced head on.

The Palace Is the Place

The sun has officially risen on a day of fasting and yet the smell of freshly baked bread lures Leili and Hooman into a small bakery with a tandoor built right into the side of the mountain.

"It's the first day of Ramadan. We shouldn't . . . ," Leili giggles. "You look like a naughty schoolboy, Hooman."

He grins at her, tucks the sheet of hot bread under his arm and beckons her to follow him behind a large rock where no one sees them pull apart the hot bread and ravenously stuff it into their mouths.

They leave their hiding spot and cautiously navigate their way down a steep and narrow street of steps brushing the evidence of their impropriety off their clothes as they go. The slight humming of cars and an occasional honk warns them of their proximity to the city. They pause for a minute before moving on to meet the coming day.

"Where's the palace?" Leili asks, looking around.

"Across the street." Hooman points toward a grassy hill nestled in a patch of pine trees presided over by a two-story modernist cement building decorated in blue-and-turquoise tiles.

"It looks more like a cultural center," Leili comments.

"The queen felt most comfortable in museums," Hooman quips.

The palace guard informs them that the café opens at 10:00 A.M., but that they are welcome to visit the Niavaran Palace Museum at 9:00—in ten minutes.

"We have an hour to kill before meeting Nima," Leili says. "Why not?"

Leili and Hooman are the only ones on the Persian tour, which weaves through the Queen's office, with its gorgeous emerald curtains and French rolltop writing desk, the Shah's sitting room, the hunting room, where animal heads restored by the artifice of taxidermy are mounted above rows of neatly stacked rifles, and the game room, where the smell of Cuban cigars still lingers about the card and billiard tables—gambling is strictly forbidden in the Islamic Republic. In the opulent red-velvet dining hall, a black-and-white photo of starving Iranians gathered around a cauldron of soup is set amidst the fine bone china engraved with the Pahlavi crest.

"Nice tactic," Hooman comments.

The last room is dedicated to Ferdowsi's *Shahnameh*, The Book of Kings, or as described on the makeshift board, "The saga of the Sassanian kings, told in mythic proportions akin to the Odyssey."

"Five years ago they wouldn't have allowed any pre-Islamic monarchial history in here, even mythology."

"Why now?" Leili asks.

"Look at the three groups behind us—all foreigners. We're the only ones on the Farsi tour."

Leili buys old postcards of the palace for Saqi in the museum store and then joins Hooman on a bench of old grandfathers wearing fedoras and reciting poetry.

"Look down there." Leili points to a small Frank Lloyd Wright–inspired wood-and-glass building nestled in the pine grove.

"That's the café," Hooman says. We should head down, Nima's waiting."

The only sound in the pine grove is of birds and a nearby chair that scrapes across the cobblestone of the café's patio, where tables and chairs have been arranged around an oblong pond.

Beneath the scum of the slimy green pond, life appears in darts of gold and orange fish.

"So this is what happens to the Nowruz fish—abandoned to the palace pond," Leili says.

"You saw that I still have mine," Hooman reassures.

They sit at a table facing the goldfish pond and wait for the waiter. They are one of three tables of patrons. Across the patio is a young couple; she's dressed in a pretty floral print scarf and he's wearing a gray suit. The woman coyly stirs her straw, pretending not to notice her drink at all. She stares into the face of the man across from her as if he is the most interesting person in the world.

"First date," Leili whispers. Hooman laughs.

The man is explaining every single computer-programming book he has ever read. The woman just barely lifts her drink to her lips every time there's a short pause but then puts it back down when he continues.

"That poor woman is dying of thirst," Leili says.

"It's her choice," Nima says gruffly.

Hooman looks up at him.

Leili smiles. But he doesn't return her smile.

"I have half a mind to walk over to her and tell her that she isn't fooling anyone but herself, and that she's in for a life of boredom and suicide if she continues to allow him to speak," Leili jokes, trying to lighten the somber mood Nima has brought with him to the table.

"That's a little extreme," Nima says.

"Check out the foreigners; they're more interesting," Hooman suggests.

"Looks like she's been shopping all over Iran," Leili says of the woman who is swathed in a long flouncy red, green and yellow skirt that is intricately splattered with tiny mirror-beads. It's a skirt traditionally worn by women who work the rice fields in the Caspian. Her orange-and-red tribal scarf comes from ethnic Arab women clear on the other side of the country, in the South, near the Gulf.

"He looks like Lawrence of Arabia," Hooman chuckles. The man is dressed in khakis, hiking boots and a long-sleeved Oxford shirt.

"She's the one with a scarf wrapped around her head like a Bedouin," Leili notes.

Their waiter stands patiently poised with his little notepad and pen, pretending to take interest in where the woman is emphatically pointing to in her travel guide.

"Like Lawrence himself pointing to a map of the desert," Hooman says, laughing.

"Bami-yeh," the woman says slowly and carefully.

"He hasn't a clue," the man says in English.

"But it's in the glossary," she says, quoting, "A sumptuous deep-fried, honey dipped, traditional Persian delicacy. It comes highly recommended and can be found in bakeries and traditional tea houses in Tehran."

"No bamiyeh," the waiter insists.

Leili giggles. "We should help and translate. We're being mean."

"We're being sane," Hooman says.

"Had there been a café here during the Shah's time they would've served exactly what they serve here now: espresso and Danish pastries," Nima remarks.

"The Shah's parties were catered by Maxim's in Paris," Hooman whispers.

"Bamiyeh," the tourist repeats loudly.

"We don't have any," the waiter says in Persian.

"How can he not know what bamiyeh is?" she asks her partner. He looks up from his English language *Tehran Times* and shrugs his shoulders.

The waiter looks at Leili and gives her an exasperated and apologetic look. He finally walks over to their table and says, "I am sorry it took so long, these tourists . . . "

"No problem," Nima says. "A cappuccino and two espressos, please." He waits for the waiter to leave before saying, "It's killing me."

"What is?" Leili asks.

"Arezoo seems to have dropped off the face of the earth. Every time I call her phone, it's off. It's been three days since . . . Are you sure she never gave either of you a home number or an address?"

"No," Leili says. "I didn't realize how little we knew about her. I feel terrible."

The waiter comes with the coffee and Nima downs his and pushes the cup back toward the waiter.

Hooman raises his eyebrows. Nima sits back in his chair. His eyes are bloodshot, his foot taps at high speed as he takes Hooman's espresso and stirs a load of sugar into it.

"Enough sugar. How about some real food? When was the last time you slept?" Hooman asks.

Nima pushes the ashtray toward Hooman when he finishes his espresso.

"I quit."

"Again?"

Hooman carefully says, "She may have left town with her boyfriend."

Nima doesn't answer. He stares out at the grove.

"It's been days."

"I've been calling you every day, and you didn't pick up until last night," Hooman reminds him. "What we went through was traumatic. Had Leili and I not been together these past days it would have been really tough. I'm glad you're not isolating your-self anymore . . . and I don't think Arezoo is either. I'm sorry, Nima, but you have to let her go."

"What if something happened to her? What if someone mur-dered that guy?"

"OK, now you are seriously hallucinating. Lack of sleep, food—Nima, he overdosed," Hooman reminds him.

"And where the hell is Kamran? He hasn't been by the paint-ball club or the gym. I've looked everywhere, asked everyone."

"I don't know," Hooman says with finality. "When you went back, did you go back down? Did you lock up?"

Nima looks away.

"Nima?" Hooman prods.

"Arezoo had my key. I gave it to her a couple of months ago when she offered to lock up for me one night."

Hooman and Leili glance at each other.

"Listen," Hooman starts carefully.

"I can't, not anymore." Nima stands, throws some money down on the table and quickly walks away.

بسم الله الرحمن الرحيم

In the Name of God

I'm working on dialogue. I'm terrible at dialogue:
  "Did you shoot anyone?"
  "Would it make a difference? Whether I killed someone else or my-self? Is suicide murder? Is killing in war murder? Where do you draw the line?"

Sunday, no word from Arezoo.
I'm afraid of losing the only friends I've ever loved.

Rewrite . . . make all past action present. Remember what Benjamin says, I have it marked, it's important, p. 147, Reflections: *"The concept of the epic theater, originated by Brecht . . . indicates above all that this theater desires an audience that is relaxed and follows the action without strain."*
Follows the action without strain? I need to rethink my genre.

An explosion that happens in the theater, unlike an explosion in war, must happen in the head of the spectator as a direct result of the script. But how?
Arezoo once described waiting for a scud missile to hit her street. I was too afraid of her back then to ask if this actually happened to her. She couldn't have been very old, even by the end of the war.
She said: "Your first instinct is relief, but then, before the tingling has stopped and the blood rushes back into your limbs and you have

even tried standing or stretching your legs that have been folded for God knows how long, before your muscles even begin to make that necessary step away from safety and back to life, you realize that someone else died instead of you." Arezoo's face was so still.

Shit, this changes everything. Survival mode erases identity. You could be anyone. Or maybe danger emphasizes identity; it shapes it and gives contours to what we are not—those things outside of ourselves that become a threat to our very lives and sanity. People relied on the war for their identity. What now?

Rehabilitation

The sudden scent of Caspian orange blossoms, the jungle of trees and undeveloped space disorient them as they drive along the dirt path toward the palace. They park, get out of the car and shake and stretch off the seven hours of the twisty Chalus Road that cuts through the mountains between the Tehran valley, the lush green rice terraces and tea fields and the Caspian seaside town of Ramsar, where the mountains dead-end into the sea.

"This doesn't look like a summer palace—are you sure we're in the right spot?" Leili asks.

"Doesn't meet with your approval? Not big enough?" Hooman jokes.

"It's a stately summer hunting home," Nima says, as if reading a guidebook description.

"Why would Arezoo want to meet here?" Leili asks.

"God knows," says Nima.

"I don't get it."

"I've told you everything—she texted me to meet her in Ramsar by the Shah's summer palace and asked if I'd take her to my villa in Babolsar. She asked me to bring you two along. I dialed back immediately and her phone was already shut off."

"Are we just leaving the car here?" Leili asks as Nima walks ahead along a gravel path skirting the main entrance to the palace. "Shouldn't a palace have a parking lot?" Leili adds.

"Apparently not," Nima answers without turning his head.

"I smell the sea," Hooman says.

"It's crazy beautiful here—it's so lush and green."

"I feel so disoriented in this part of the Caspian, I feel so . . ." Nima pauses to look around. "I hope she comes. What if someone else texted me from her phone? No voice, no positive ID. What if this is a prank?"

"Then we'll meet them and get to the bottom of it," Hooman says.

"What do we say to her?" Nima asks. "She just disappears . . ."

"Hello?" Leili suggests.

"Let her do the talking," Hooman suggests, and then, "There she is." He waves to her in the distance.

Arezoo walks along the palace periphery wearing the same clothes and carrying the same backpack and purse as the night that they last saw her over three weeks ago.

"You're all here," Arezoo says breathlessly. "Thanks," she mutters, "for coming." She looks at the gravel driveway and starts to say, "I . . ." Her eyes well up. She bows her head.

"It's OK," Hooman says, "We've all had a hard time since . . . there's no rush to talk."

"Are you all right?" Nima asks. "Are you hurt?"

She shakes her head without looking up at him.

Arezoo's shyness is as out of character as her silence. Even her voice has changed in the past weeks, or maybe Leili's just not used to hearing it above ground.

Arezoo looks up at them and says, "Thank you for coming. I would have run as far away from me as possible if I were you."

"No, you wouldn't have," Nima insists. He opens the front door of the car for her, but Arezoo climbs into the back seat. "Leili," she says, patting the seat next to her. Leili smiles. She's never been Arezoo's first choice to sit next to. She climbs in and takes Arezoo's hand. A tear runs down Arezoo's face. She wipes it quickly and Leili is relieved that not everything about her has changed.

"We missed you," Leili says.

Arezoo looks out the window and falls silent.

"You'll like this drive," Nima says, "It's all sea from here to Babolsar."

Arezoo clears her throat but doesn't answer.

They leave the palace and head into town for torsh kabob, kabobs smothered in the famous Ramsar pomegranate sauce and a box of *kuluche,* the quintessential Caspian coconut cookie.

They drive for three hours along the lush green Caspian coastline, West to East, listening to a soft mix of classical Persian music, Leonard Cohen and Persian fusion: Mahsa Vahdat, Rana Farhan and Mamak Khadem.

"I love her voice," Arezoo says looking out the window.

"She lives in Tehran now," Nima says. Arezoo doesn't comment. Her eyes are focused out the window on the makeshift tourist shops that line the road, each one like the next: woven baskets, large wooden spoons and colorful balloons hang from the rafters. Scattered in between them are kabob stands where men smoke water pipes while they wait for skewers of fresh lamb's liver and heart. Every so often they pass a lone man or woman with a herd of brightly colored toy rocking horses.

"Are they papier-mâché?" Leili asks.

"Want one?" Hooman jokes.

"That bright orange one."

"I wasn't serious," Hooman says.

"We can put it in the back," Nima suggests, already slowing down, braking and putting the car in reverse.

Leili squeals and turns in her seat to help navigate.

Nima pulls up alongside the Caspian couple and their toy horses. The man's shirt flaps like a sail in the wind that might blow off were it not pinned down by his pinstriped vest. His wife's baggy calico dress and white cotton headscarf puff and billow like pillowcases on a clothesline. They look like real shepherds against the backdrop of the lush green and brown Alborz Mountains, standing stoically amidst their inanimate and unnaturally bright herd.

"We'll take two," Nima tells the man. "The orange one and . . ." turning to Arezoo, "and?"

"The red one." She smiles for the first time.

Nima loads the horses into the back of the Land Rover.

"Can we listen to the Rahna Farhan song again?" Arezoo asks when they're back on the road.

"Which one?" Nima asks, one hand on the wheel, the other fumbling with his mp3 player.

"Untangled," says Arezoo.

"You mean 'Tangled'? Nima asks.

Arezoo laughs. "Yeah, the one where she's trying to get untangled."

An overgrown garden of wildflowers and pretty green weeds skirts Nima's family's villa.

"You said your family had a cabin," Hooman comments.

"It's wood, A-frame."

"It's huge," Hooman says.

They park next to outdoor shower stalls covered in overgrown ivy and termite holes.

"Do you use these?" Leili asks.

"We did when I was a child. Back then they were curtained by walls of pink and orange bougainvillea. It felt so refreshing to wash off the salty Caspian seawater after a long day swimming," Nima says.

"Women can't swim in the sea," Leili says.

"Sure they can. There's a curtain that stretches for miles into the sea to segregate it. But it's not advisable."

"Why?" asks Hooman.

"It's polluted, the beach has eroded, it's all rock," Nima answers.

"What's the point?" Arezoo says.

They smile at her, happy that she's more herself.

A young freckled, green-eyed local girl with long red braids that hang out of the sides of her blue calico chador greets them at the door. "Welcome," she says cheerfully.

"Where are your parents?" Nima asks her.

"They're at home. My father says he'll come by to give you a report from the grove. There's a basket of oranges on the table. They sent me to cook and clean for you while you're here," she announces proudly.

"Thank you," Nima says. "Don't you have school?"

"We're on break sir, it's a religious holiday." She blushes deeply at his blunder.

"Of course," Nima says and signals for his guests to enter the villa.

In the morning, for lack of a better plan or any plan at all, they take a motorboat tour of the canals. The little motorboat bobs up and down on mossy waves created by a stormy sea. It's too loud for conversation, and so the four of them sit silently with their thoughts. They study the lily pads and their precarious purple flowers that fight to stay afloat.

The day is spent reading in the garden. In the early evening they amble through the tiny bazaar, where they buy plastic beach balls and bamboo mats they won't use; a porcelain tea set hostess gift for Nima's mom; locally harvested tea; and walnut cookies for friends.

They carry their bags to the car and walk out to the sea to sit along the shore.

Leili is the first to bring up the theater. "Hooman, you should write about the war."

"Isn't it too close to home?" Nima asks protectively.

"It depends on whose story we tell," he answers tentatively.

"Not mine," says Arezoo.

"You already told me about the missile. It's a good story," Hooman reminds her.

"Yeah, but I didn't tell you that while your family was defending our country the people we lived with were taping black construction paper to their basement windows so that the Komiteh wouldn't see boys and girls dancing together."

"Guilty comparisons. We were kids," Hooman assures her.

"People you lived with?" Leili asks.

"My family lived in the basement of rich folks. My mom did their cooking and cleaning. Sometimes she took me with her upstairs to help out at parties. The boys were always nice to me and pretended I was a guest, even though I was young and out of place. The girls were mean and never spoke to me."

"Sorry," Leili says lamely.

"The missile?" Nima asks.

"Oh yeah. The war was almost over and we were oblivious to the outside world—screaming to a Deep Purple song at the top of our lungs, jumping around, sweating. The teenage boys were flirting and fearless. Suddenly we realized that our voices were the only ones still singing—electricity blackout. Saddam was overhead. It's like the night held its breath and listened with us. Was this the end?" Arezoo doesn't look at Hooman as she speaks.

"What were you feeling?" Hooman looks at her tenderly.

"Nothing. Dead empty, like a soundless cave. Then the bomb dropped. Bang. Deafening. Then silence says you survived but that surely someone else, maybe right next door, or as far away as the school playground, is dead."

"Don't stop," Hooman says.

She looks at Hooman, who stares out at the sea, smoking and listening.

"The first time we went down to our practice space it reminded me of that basement." She pauses briefly and says, "I felt both a sense of relief and of horror." She puts her head in her hands and cries.

Hooman clears his throat and says, "We just wrote our play."

The next evening they stop along the shore to watch a group of women form a prayer line along the edge of the sea. The women motion for them to move along.

"The women can stay," they say in their singsong Caspian accents. Then they turn back to each other and giggle in *Gilaki* about the boys and girls walking together. Arezoo points to the makeshift curtain that blocks them from men praying alongside them, present but unseen.

"Woops," says Nima and leads them to a giant rock where they can sit and watch the sea.

Eclipsed by the dying light, the rising and prostrating shadows of the praying women dance across the rocks like black ghosts floating on the horizon.

"It's so peaceful—I can almost feel the prayer," Leili says softly.

"It's been a long time since I've seen anyone pray," Arezoo says.

"Where's Hooman?" Leili looks around her.

"He's snuck off to the pier," says Nima. "Not in the mood for the spectacle of organized religion. He's gone to meditate."

"And you?" Leili asks Nima.

"I pray with my dad, for my dad," he answers.

"I want to go to the mosque," says Leili. They give her a surprised look.

"What for?" asks Arezoo. She rubs her arms against the chill.

"I've never really been to one," she says.

"How is that possible? They force us into the mosque at every opportunity," Nima says, looking at Leili as if meeting her for the first time.

"I'm Christian," Leili says, "I'm sure Hooman mentioned it?"

"He did, but you still grew up here?"

"I'm allowed to opt out of religious school trips."

Arezoo immediately agrees to go with her.

"Really?" asks Nima, surprised.

"Why not? Let's go," says Arezoo.

Leili walks to the pier to summon Hooman. She finds him sitting cross-legged, eyes closed. His faith defies explanation. There are no guides or laws. He's told her many times that God is everywhere: in the rain, the foam of the green sea, freshly baked bread and the swish of a chador.

Hooman opens his eyes; a faint smile plays on his lips. He looks peaceful, rested. Leili whispers, "Was it easy to learn?"

"There's nothing to learn. You just tap into something that's already there," Hooman answers.

The women borrow prayer chadors from the villa and head back out for the evening prayer.

They ride the bus standing chador to chador in the women's section for one short stop. Leili, self-conscious in her chador, looks down at the other hems that glide across the floorboards of the bus.

The day draws its last breath and exhales a gust of cold, dark wind that pulls at their chadors and threatens to steal away with them. Leili turns her back to secure her chador as night falls slowly to its knees.

The large crystal chandeliers at the entrance of the mosque bob brightly in the wind. Kabob stands dot the walkway toward the grand blue honeycombed-tile entrance to the mosque where families gather festively, picnic baskets and duffels in hand, looking for friends and relatives.

"It would be fun to spend the night here with all the pilgrims," Leili says at the mosque entrance.

"I guess," Arezoo says off-handedly.

They enter through the women's door and circle the saint's tomb, stopping to pray and kiss and tie strings around the gilded cage.

Arezoo looks into the crowd of men separated by Plexiglas. Leili follows her gaze to an Afghani Sufi with a long thin beard, a high wool cone-shaped cap and flowing cape.

"He reminds me of my father," Arezoo says. The man is tall and thin and his face is raised as if to implore the heavens.

"Where is he?" Leili asks.

"No longer." Arezoo shakes her head. "I wish he were alive." Tears well up in her eyes. "We could finally be covered by the same dome and protected by the same God," she says.

"You are," says Leili.

"I've felt so betrayed by God. I needed his protection," Arezoo cries softly.

"I'm sure he's looking down on you now with pride," Leili says.

"I doubt it," Arezoo says. "God doesn't approve of me."

"I meant your dad," Leili says.

"Him too," says Arezoo, "He was a laborer, an Afghan. He killed himself to put food on our table. In Afghanistan he was a teacher of Persian poetry and music. He met my mother in Tehran. She's Afghan too but was born and raised here. She brought me up with a perfect Tehran accent—no one ever knew. He tutored me every evening, he put me through school, and what did I do? I betrayed him."

"How? You have a B.A., you're doing theater, you sing and you're a hard worker." Leili's not even sure what Arezoo does for a living.

"I'm a burnout."

"Don't be silly," Leili puts her arm around Arezoo.

Arezoo moves away. "Leili, I betrayed all of you. I can't tell

Nima and Hooman. I'm too ashamed—they've done so much for me over the years . . . I need a female friend."

Leili stares at Arezoo.

"Listen, don't talk . . . It's my fault the soldier died in our practice space," Arezoo says and waits for Leili to react.

"Go on."

"The needles were my boyfriend's . . . and . . ." Arezoo swallows, "mine."

"Yours!"

"Shhh . . ." Arezoo gives her an unnecessary warning, for the mosque is as loud as a schoolyard. She looks around anyway before continuing: "It all started when Kamran met my boyfriend at one of our silly voice practices. Kamran and I were practicing at a studio at Farabi Film Center and my boyfriend wanted in on the free studio space. We all went back to his place to smoke pot. Kamran offered to score us some coke. He was bragging about all his dealer connections and how they could have a safe buying spot if only I'd get them a key." Arezoo stops and looks away.

"And?" Leili asks.

"I asked Nima for his. Kamran had no idea what he was getting into. My friends like heroin. Kamran freaked out, they got into a big fight and my boyfriend punched him. That's when Kamran stopped coming to practice—he was too scared."

"And you? Weren't you scared?"

"All the time. But I was hooked. I tried the stuff at a party once, a few months back, and that was all it took for me." Arezoo puts her face in her hands.

"What happened?"

"I don't know. I haven't seen either of them since before that night. I got really sick and I was trying to stop . . . I didn't go with him the last time he tried to score, the night the soldier must have . . . I'd never seen the guy shoot up. He sold us drugs. He came in quickly, did the handover and then left. He was border patrol and had tons of confiscated stuff from Afghanistan." Arezoo pauses to look around before continuing to whisper. "My boyfriend must have let him in and then . . ." Arezoo's lips tremble; she fights hard to hold back the tears. "He must have OD'd and my boyfriend just left him . . . or . . . I don't know . . ." Arezoo is shaking.

"Are you still . . . ?"

"Using? No. I ran away that night after you left. This woman at a party gave me her number one night—told me to call her if I ever wanted to quit and couldn't." Arezoo puts her head in her hands and cries.

"It's OK," Leili says softly.

Arezoo isn't the only one crying. The mosque is full of people who have come from all corners of the Province to implore God, to thank him, to take comfort and to petition—some with tears of joy and others with tears of sorrow.

"I'm OK. I'm going to be all right. Thank God, for some odd reason I kept that number in my wallet. I called that woman from a phone booth near the theater. And she came. In the middle of the night she came for me. That's what ex-addicts do for each other, Leili. She drove all night up that crazy, windy Chalus Road to take me to a rehab near the palace. She insisted I get as far away from Tehran as possible. I texted Nima when my time was ending because I don't want that life or to return to those people. The only goodness in my life is you, Hooman and Nima." Arezoo looks up toward the mirror-tiled ceiling and says, "I need to find some faith. When I heard them say this in rehab, the first person I thought of was Hooman. His faith must be unshakable—to believe in God's protection after the wrath the war brought down on his family."

"He says that God disagrees with most of what's done in his name," Leili says.

"I need to forgive God, too," Arezoo says. "I need Hooman to show me how."

"How to?"

"To believe. To forgive."

"He wants us to believe in ourselves."

"No. I'm done with me. I need to believe in a power greater than myself," Arezoo says. She hugs Leili tightly and pulls her up. "Thank you, Leili joon." Arezoo then wiggles out of her embrace as if to say good-bye.

"Where are you going?" Leili asks, concerned.

"I have to find the perfect place," Arezoo says.

"Perfect place for what?" asks Leili.

"To pray," Arezoo says.

They weave in and out of rooms separated by large Persian rugs that hang from the twenty-foot ceiling as doors. In and out through the labyrinth of twinkling mirrored walls to the outdoor courtyard with its blue-and-yellow honeycomb-tiled fountains. The Caspian women with their calico chadors smile at them as they pass. They step over dining, praying and sleeping families. Arezoo finally finds a spot and sits down next to a young woman who has placed her prayer stone and rug in front of her. She trades a black street chador for a cream-colored calico prayer chador.

"I'm going to wander around," Leili says, worried that she won't even be able to mime the prayer once it begins.

"Don't worry," Arezoo whispers, reading her mind. "In a mosque this large and crowded no one will notice the nondevout." She winks and giggles, "Look, Leili, her chador's inside-out." Arezoo points out the woman's secret sign that she's an available *sigeh*—a woman to marry for a night to ninety-nine years.

Leili wonders if the form of prayer, the rising and falling, is ingrained in Hooman's body forever. She heard somewhere that habit forms belief, but she disagrees. She's kneeled and crossed herself for years without faith.

In the prayer hall the men sit cross-legged and erect, patiently awaiting the arrival of the mullah. In the family room a young college student sketches a stranger's face, while a father reads the Quran to his children. Grandchildren crawl over their sleeping grandmother and in the process transform her into a mammoth rock covered by a black chador.

Leili sits and tries to meditate, but she can't stop imagining Arezoo shooting up. She tries to concentrate on her breath coming in and going out and when that doesn't work she counts her breath, but still, the image of Arezoo's desperate and pale face the night they found the soldier keeps flowing back in until she finally hears the tapping of the microphone that precedes the call of the faithful to prayer.

She's entirely out of her element and so she delicately untangles her numb legs and carefully stands. She shakes her legs until the blood flows back and then gingerly steps between prostrated bodies all the way to the shoe depository where men wait to enter, shoes in hand. The women enter delicately as if under cover, holding bags, children, books and the corner of a chador bunched up in a single hand while agilely stepping out of their shoes. The slip of a hand reveals a wedding ring or a schoolbook, groceries or a bundled child hidden warmly in the fold of his mother's moving tent. Leili watches the eyes, and the eyes watch her. Some are heavily lined in black kohl, others framed in wire-rimmed glasses; serious expressions and teasing smiles stare back at her.

بسم الله الرحمن الرحيم

In the Name of God

Carl Jung told an alcoholic that the answer to his problem was God. According to Arezoo and her new "clean" friends, Jung said an addict is someone who has lost her spiritual center and in her search for God turned to drugs.

Listening to Arezoo talk made me think about our odd geographical luck. First we are on the good old Silk Road, which has placed us squarely in the middle of every historic drug market. What a laugh. The world's strictest religious state has the highest per-capita opiate consumption in the world. Goes to show that if addiction is a loss of spirituality, then religion and spirituality are not the same thing. Then we're also part of the hippy trail where every spiritual seeker, from college dropouts to famous philosophers like Henri Corbin, came to grapple with the question of religion and spirituality for modern times. Of course we Iranians took it a step further in 1979 and brought it into the political sphere and destroyed it for everyone.

Our religious revolution caused the world to distrust religion, though you wouldn't know it now in the US, where Christian revival movements are booming—especially in politics—or so I read. It's still hip here to think of Americans as profane, whatever that means. Leili is reading a self-help book and the author is a "pastor" (another word for ayatollah??) at a church in California (so it may not really be a church at all and she may not really be learned in religious exegesis). We share with the West a spiritual thirst. And just like in the West, this thirst is sometimes quenched by drugs and alcohol, despite our mighty strong prohibition.

Nightmares are contagious. Is addiction?

Clean. *I don't like this choice of word. Arezoo was clean even when she was doing drugs.*

Recovery. *She says she's recovering her true self. But it really sounds more like a recrafting, or a crafting of a self, the way an actor works to create and bring to life a character. She said it's different. It's a rebirth of a character that already existed. And besides, according to Arezoo it involves faith and another's help . . . and this is what scares me. It sounds just like religion—adding an intermediary with rules and regulations between yourself and God.*

Arezoo tells me not to intellectualize her disease, but I don't know how else to understand it. It's the body or the mind, and since my body would literally crumble under that kind of research, it will have to be the secondary organ that explores this terrain, the lesser one . . . my mind. And it's not like there's a lot of information on it here, the only thing I've found was in a philosophy book, of all places. Philosopher Gilles Deleuze, a friend of Michel Foucault (who sat, no, practically kneeled at Khomeini's feet in Neuphel le Chateau where Khomeini was exiled to just before the Revolution) muses that he used to drink a lot but had to stop for health reasons. He says, "We are trying to extract from love all possession, all identification, to become capable of loving. . . . We are trying to extract from alcohol the life, which it contains, without drinking." He uses acting as an example and a scene in a Henry Miller play—getting drunk on pure water.

Acting is its own kind of extraction. It reminds me of Stanislavski's idea of "acting as if." Acting as if we are free. We extract the real or the false, depending on our intentions, and we can then experience drink without drinking, freedom without democracy, love without touching, life without fail.

Tehran Times

For a time Leili worked nightly on her father's portrait, but then rehearsals grew more and more intense and she saw him less and less and soon the painting faded right into the wall—until tonight, when she stumbles on it in the dark. Every angle is wrong. Her father refused to pose, so she did the painting from memory and in the end it is only his abstraction that she has captured.

She kicks it aside. "This will be his only trace," she says to the night.

Saqi called Leili home from the Caspian. "Your father's in the hospital," she simply said. "He drank too much and waited too long to go for help and now the doctors are keeping him in the hospital overnight for tests."

Leili doesn't turn on the light or take off her rupush. She is too exhausted to prepare for bed. She sits down on the floor next to the painting, with her back against the wall, and looks out of her bedroom window at the moonlit street.

"Uncle Jehan called," Saqi says, opening the bedroom door and sticking her head in.

"He never calls," Leili says.

"It's expensive to call from Europe, phone lines are tapped, and besides, what's there to say?"

"Lots," Leili whispers. "How did he know about Dad?"

"I called him . . . ," Saqi admits.

Her uncle left without warning a decade ago. Despite Internet cafés and mobile phones, her father blamed bad phone lines for the lack of calls. He saw slow bandwidth and broken lines clogging communication the way bumps and potholes have done traffic for the past thirty years. Maybe her father was right. Her uncle offered to take Leili with him to Sweden—he thought her parents were making a big mistake not to get her out.

"Give up my child?" Saqi cried in the salon that night. Leili was watching, listening safely hidden behind the large door as the three adults debated her fate.

"I can't," Saqi said. And that was the end of that.

"What are you thinking about?" Saqi asks.

"Baba's photos," Leili answers.

"Leili, I'm really sorry you had to come home. I know how much your friends mean to you. Is the one who was sick better?"

"Arezoo . . . yes, she's fine," Leili says, getting up and walking toward her mother. She gives Saqi a hug and says, "Baba means a lot to me, too."

"I know. But you have to let him go. I've been so pleased to watch you get out more. It's true we've missed you, but this is your time, your prime . . . you must live your life now," Saqi says.

Leili breaks away from her mother.

"Where to?" Saqi asks.

"The darkroom," Leili says.

Saqi stretches out her arms. Leili embraces her mother again and cries.

Leili spends the evening in the red glow of her father's old darkroom, looking through already-fading pictures he took before the Revolution, when her parents were still students, well before Leili was born. There is a stack of Saqi: sporting argyle socks on a hike in Damavand, less rotund and decked out in a sequined dress at a late-night cabaret, in black capri pants and bowling shoes at Bowling-e Abdo, in her ice skates and red ear-muffs at The Ice Castle.

In the morning she sets her easel close to the mirror and mixes her paints: warm browns for her eyes and hair, auburn for her highlights, a milky coffee for her skin, and pale pink for her lips. She tries to look at her portrait objectively before adding small lines around her light brown oval-shaped eyes and shading her eyebrows darker than they really are. Her large triangular nose takes center stage above wide lips and high Scandinavian cheek-bones. She chisels a long, even line into her forehead, like a Qajar princess's unibrow, and accentuates strong, angular features that she wishes she had. A Japanese calligraphy brush creates thick dark-black lashes. The result is less Leili and more a Picasso mistress.

She paints herself seated in her father's armchair. Picasso once said, "When I paint a woman in an armchair, I am painting old age and death." Unlike Picasso's women, she can't bring herself back to life in the forefront of her own canvas. Instead, she has perfected the art of losing herself in the background.

"Simple lines," her teacher always said.

Her paints ooze together on the plastic pallet; she doesn't have the patience for painting. She wants to paint over wet lay-ers and risk destroying her work. If he had been a painter, her father would have waited for the layers to dry before moving on. In lieu of the darkroom timer he gave her as a child she wishes that he had passed on his patience—the ability to concentrate, to lose himself in the light of his cigarette. His patience wasn't natural but a side effect of a self-imposed loneliness—she knows this and yet she envies it. Painting is an aloneness with oneself that does not inherently imply loneliness; she is only beginning to understand the difference. She stares blankly out the window for inspiration and thinks of the theater, of the human body in motion resisting the act of becoming still, set and framed, of Hooman, Nima and Arezoo waiting to catch her in the dark. By nightfall her canvas is rolled up and pushed into the trash next to which she lies on the floor, stretching her body—the sculptural self-portrait well in progress.

Fireflies

"Hooman!" Leili waylays Hooman, who is about to cross the street.

"What's wrong?" he asks demurely.

"You know damn well. It's not safe."

"The theater?" Leili nods. "Nima's kept an eye on it. Checked it out every night for the past month." He takes her elbow and steers her away from the curb. The mad evening rush of pedestrians is made worse by presidential election campaigners.

"There's nothing, no indication of anything. Mashti says they came and took the body and sealed the place with the same lock. Even Arezoo admitted to letting the guy in. The needles were hers, Leili; no one else has been in there since. It's safe."

"It's haunted."

"Leili, don't be silly."

Leili looks across the street.

"We would have known by now if anyone else was using the place," Hooman insists. "Including a ghost."

"Not necessarily. What about Kamran?"

"He's safely tucked away in rehab in Switzerland. I doubt he'll be back."

"He may have said something. They could be waiting for our return—for the most optimal moment . . ."

"When we are all writhing around on the floor?" He laughs.

Leili doesn't respond. "Well, then, they have something to look forward to." He pulls a cigarette from a pack and lights it.

"What about Arezoo?"

"It's her idea. She insists. She went back with Nima a few times and says she's fine. It's something she feels she needs to do, to face."

"And why the middle of the night? You haven't forgotten that we're under a curfew have you?"

"The audience is exhausted, less resistant, and the Komiteh, not to mention campaigners, are asleep." Hooman takes slow, even puffs of his cigarette while people move around them frenetically. "And, there is almost no chance that we'll be caught in the middle of the night. And . . . as Arezoo pointed out, people can come to see our play without missing anything at the University Theater Festival. We'll send out a word-of-mouth announcement about the performance twenty-four hours ahead."

A cabbie interrupts them: "You coming or going?" he asks. They've somehow found themselves in the rush-hour taxi line on the sidewalk.

"We should try the bus line next," she jokes. "More privacy," she adds as they walk toward the juice stand. She's silent for a moment and then says, "Seriously, Hooman, you're asking us to expose our practice space, the only one we have available to us, and at the same time run the risk of shutting down our show on opening night just to perform for a handful of people? In the meantime we will most likely be reprimanded, in God knows what way. You *do* realize that the presidential elections are in a couple of days?"

"What difference have elections ever made? No one takes them seriously."

"The government's sensitive around election time. People are busy campaigning this year. It's pretty serious, Hooman. Look around you: there are banners everywhere. Besides, what if no one comes?"

"It doesn't matter how many people are in the audience. Sometimes it's only one person who makes a difference."

"What do you mean?" asks Leili. This time they reach the front of the line much faster.

"Leili, they're waiting."

"I . . ." She looks down at the sidewalk.

"Come?" Hooman asks. When she doesn't answer him, Hooman turns away. She looks up and watches him walk toward the fountain and to Nima, who smiles and waves to him from across the street.

That's love, she thinks, and darts across the street toward the theater.

بسم الله الرحمن الرحيم

In the Name of God

I've been thinking a lot about stories. It would be so much easier to just write and publish and not have to perform. The performance adds the danger element. At least with writing you can change your name. When you get out there with your body you're trapped.

Stories. Why are they so damn dangerous? They can create and destroy a moral order. They tell us of origins, they give us belief systems and transport us to places we've never been before and give us experiences we hope to never have.

Storytelling began as primitive science called mythology when we didn't have the proper science to explain things like thunder or why volcanoes erupt. So we came up with myths like Vulcan, the blacksmith in Greek mythology who made thunderbolts for Zeus. As he made the thunderbolts, flames sparked from the tip of the mountain under which he lived (a volcano). In our own mythology, Kaveh the blacksmith may be responsible for Mt. Damavand's fire. Stories can still be scientific; they can still be useful. When we can't tell things as they are, we can use stories. When we have messed up politically and need to save face, our job or our country, we tell stories. When we teach our children and we don't want to blame or stigmatize them, we use stories. When we are in recovery, spiritual or otherwise, we tell our story.

Once you let go of a story and it gets out into the public and circulates, it changes and there's nothing you can do to reel it back in.

Walter Benjamin understands the power of a story. He says, "By basing their historical tales on a divine plan of salvation—an inscruta-

ble one—*they have from the very start lifted the burden of demonstrable explanation from their own shoulders." Salvation. Martyrdom is a great story; you can't touch it. Did Benjamin live here in Iran?*

I need to be careful not to abuse my role as storyteller. It's a powerful role. But it's also up to folks to interpret stories for themselves. That's the only way to survive—being able to read a story for what it is makes us more resilient. We have to be able to read intention so that we can decide who and when and what to trust. We are the only ones who can rebuild ourselves against this master narrative. I guess that's what Arezoo was saying: addiction, religion, politics are examples of narratives that lead us away from who we really are and ultimately from each other and God. We need to create alternative narratives. It's funny, repression can be freeing. Those of us who have had the privilege of being silenced tend to resist false stories—because we are more distrusting. We know that we are being lied to.

Been listening to a lot of Leonard Cohen. All it takes is a crack for the light to get in.

Hospital of Failed Martyrs

Leili sits by her father's hospital bed and watches his labored breath punch listlessly at his rib cage. She wants to ask him if he is afraid, if he fears death. She observes him lying on the bed like the old gnarled tree branch that she found in the Caspian. It had just rained and the wood smelled fresh and was shellacked with moisture. She dragged the smooth, shiny golden branch for a mile and made a convincing and passionate argument to Nima to put the dirty wet branch in his father's new Land Rover. They brought it to the Villa and the next day the branch dried: its color and sheen had faded and its smoothness was replaced by the dry, stiff ordinariness of firewood. She looks at her father, wanting to see the branch she found in the forest, but instead sees only the dead wood that dried up the next day.

Leili dozes off and wakes to find Hooman standing in the room.

"So this is where you've run away to." He gives her a concerned look.

"Pancreatitis."

"I'm sorry. Arezoo called me."

"Do you think he's less afraid of dying because he lacks the desire to live?" she asks.

"What makes you think he's not afraid?" he asks softly.

Leili looks down at her father; a tear trickles down her cheek.

"I don't. I just never really thought he wanted to live."

"Want a coffee? We can talk in the café?"

Leili looks down at her father, needlessly checking to see if he is watching. He has not opened his eyes since they brought him here five days ago.

"I already miss him," she says. She thinks of the delicate way he holds his exotic canary, studying the bird like a naturalist, appreciating its contours, its evolution. He is the opposite of a parlor pet owner who would simply fluff the bird's curly feathers and coax it to sing.

"I need to feed his bird," she says rising to her feet. "Who will take care of his bird?" she asks as if she too is leaving.

"You're here," Hooman says.

She takes Hooman's hand and leads him out of the room.

Outside, the night air is still and warm. Hooman lights a cigarette and takes a drag.

"He's dying."

Leili looks out across the street into the dark Tehran night where bombs have left gaping holes like dropped jaws and hollow eye sockets silenced by shock and terror. The city looks different to her from the doors of the hospital. She thinks of a suicide victim she passed earlier in the hall, dyeing the sheets red as she dies.

"There was a suicide," Leili remarks.

"The hospital of failed martyrs," Hooman says.

"Why is it that when men fail their suicide missions they return heroes and when women fail theirs they are branded insane?"

"I'd rather be insane," Hooman says. "It's much more honest."

Leili looks up at Hooman with tears in her eyes.

"I wish there was more time."

"We're not in charge of time, Leili. That's up to God."

"My father used to put me in charge of time," Leili says. "He never allowed me near the magic powders and liquids that transformed paper into pictures, but he put me in charge of the most important part of the process."

"Which was?"

"Time. He stationed me outside the darkroom door with a big silver egg-shaped timer that magically knew when the chemicals had transformed a blank piece of paper into an intricate image.

My father taught me to make my first photograph. It was a close-up of an elephant's foot at the zoo. I loved the texture of his skin, his giant glassy toenails, and the way his live flesh was so like my gray leather Mary Jane shoes. My father held the camera while I looked through the viewfinder. He showed me how to twist the lens into focus, and gently pressed my finger down on the big silver button until the pressure of our efforts made a clicking of rotating mirrors."

"Do you have these photos?" Hooman asks.

"No. Nothing turned out the way I wanted. Which is probably why I wanted to paint so badly. I wanted to make a perfect lasting image, but they all came out blurry and then faded. My father was still proud. He used to make me feel better by telling me a story that I thought he had made up especially for me. You know the one by Rumi about the elephant?" Leili cries.

"An elephant is brought to a small village under the cover of night. No one in the village has ever seen an elephant, and everyone is curious," Hooman begins.

Leili nods and blows her nose. "Keep going," she says.

"That same night a number of the villagers sneak into the place where the elephant is kept. They feel around in the dark, trying to sense this large, foreign beast. The next day, each describes the elephant. The one who touched the elephant's leg describes a column, those who touched his trunk describe a large hose, and those who touched his ears envisioned a fan." Hooman pauses before saying, "Had they each a candle they would have seen the same elephant."

بسم الله الرحمن الرحيم
In the Name of God

Jean Genet: audience = prisoners. They hold themselves prisoner by choice.

We will seat men and women next to each other. We will demand that the audience take the same risk we performers are taking. The audience should feel both fear and safety. That's what we feel every day that we are down there, every day that we survive for our art—slipping between the inside and the outside, between fear and safety.

Why should the audience sit back comfortably and watch the actors work in fear? Why should the civilians feel comfortable taking shelter while the soldiers cower in the trenches? Who are the players, and who is the audience in war? In English the battlefield is called a theater.

We'll give out more tickets than we have seats. The audience will be forced to sit knee to knee. They won't be allowed to feel comfortable (not difficult on hard cement benches).

Our play could restore sanity to those who come to sit in our shelter. Okay, so not just like that. Of course it's up to the spectators whether they'll feel protected or threatened.

When I told Leili this, she said it would be nice if something as simple as theater could wake us up from our nightmares.

Why not? Aren't you a believer? I asked her. She said she wants to believe, but she's a realist. I almost choked laughing. Leili, a realist?

She keeps asking me, Why is the audience so important? And I keep telling her that people will stay the same if given the choice. It's events that change things and theater is an event that changes the audience, who in turn will change others—mass therapy.

Leili laughed. "Do you really think we're the ones to give therapy?" Maybe she is a realist. Regardless, it's our responsibility as artists to share what we've learned, what we have, what we've been given—it's a gift. We should give it away for free.

She really has a way of making me doubt myself. Am I being too arrogant? Is this ridiculous?

I'm reading Grief Lessons: Four Plays by Euripides, *translated by Ann Carson. Carson says it best in one of her introductory essays, "Preface to Tragedy: A Curious Art Form" (great title): "Grief and rage—you need to contain that, to put a frame around it, where it can play itself out without you or your kin having to die. There is a theory that watching unbearable stories about other people lost in grief and rage is good for you—may cleanse you of darkness. Do you want to go down to the pits of yourself all alone? Not much. What if an actor could do it for you? Isn't that why they are called actors? They act for you."*

We will sacrifice ourselves to save our audience.

The Show Goes On and On

Hooman takes Leili's hand and pulls her into the landing. He shuts the door and the dark envelops them before she has a chance to look around.

"Wait, I'll be back with a candle," he says.

"Okay," Leili whispers, aware of how much her body sways in the dark. Time away from here has shifted her balance.

Hooman returns, placing one foot gingerly in front of the other. He concentrates on the candle he holds with both hands.

"Now," he says. And she follows him and the flicker of light he carries down the dark narrow staircase.

"Are you sure?"

"You're asking me now? Again?" Hooman asks.

She hesitates. "What if there's an earthquake?"

"Earthquake? After almost a year of practicing down here and you're suddenly thinking about earthquakes?"

Leili shrugs.

"In that case, you will be relieved to know that if there is an earthquake, we will die instantly, assuredly, and without pain."

"And together," says Leili.

"We die alone."

"Not if it's in the same instant," Leili insists.

"Believe what you want, if it makes you feel better, but in the end we are alone."

Leili looks longingly at the concrete walls, the benches, the practice mats and the candles that are placed in a circle as if it's her first time here. She knows it could be her last.

"I missed this place. It's so mystical." Leili looks around, trying to think of a way to describe the warmth of the candlelight and the feeling of serenity.

Hooman walks over to her and touches her face. Her cheeks are hot.

"Are you okay? You look so serious."

Her smile is unconvincing.

"The others will be here soon. I'll go see if we have an audience yet!"

"I'm coming, too." She runs after him.

The junkies and pimps retreat to their bushes like rats afraid of the Komiteh that the crowd lined up outside of the City Theater are sure to soon attract.

It hadn't occurred to Hooman that last minute word-of-mouth in a city with a population of ten million people with nothing better to do would reach more than the twenty people that they hoped to squeeze into the theater.

"You'd think that nothing else is happening in Tehran," says Arezoo. She and Nima join the mass of young people at the theater entrance.

"Nothing is," says Hooman. He nervously watches the crowd. "Aren't people too tired after voting to sit through a play at midnight?"

"We got the day off. How hard is it to cast a vote?" Nima asks, still in campaign mode.

"How should we handle all these people?" Hooman wonders aloud.

"We should give them a receipt with their place in line and allow them to come back tomorrow for the next performance. Otherwise we'll attract the Komiteh posthaste," Nima whispers.

"Who's going to call the Komiteh? The pimps and prostitutes?" Hooman laughs. He puts his hand on his forehead.

Arezoo gives him a cautionary look.

"Ok, you're right," he says. He fumbles for a cigarette and looks around.

"You could make a killing on this even if you only charged a couple of Tomans a ticket," Nima suggests.

More and more people come from the square toward the theater.

"Ever the businessman. No charge. Receipts, however, are a good idea," Hooman says.

Arezoo fishes in her purse for her journal and rips out a fistful of clean pages. She takes a red marker and writes down numbers.

"Give that to me," Hooman says. "You guys need to warm up." Nima and Arezoo disappear behind the curtain.

A man with a big bushy beard, square glasses and a black turtleneck calmly thumbs prayer beads on the periphery. He catches Hooman's eye. Hooman looks away but the man is already walking over.

"I heard about your last avant-garde attempt. I'm a critic," he says to Hooman.

"Oh," Hooman continues carefully. "We aren't inviting critics just yet. Seats are for commoners."

The man raises his eyebrows.

"We're less concerned with critical reception," Hooman clarifies, continuing, "It's a work in progress we're still practicing. You're welcome to come back later." Hooman turns to walk away. The man reaches out and grabs his shoulder. Hooman turns back.

"Look brother, there will be no later. You either give me a seat now, or you get shut down," the man tells him.

"You can't shut us down." Hooman gestures to the crowd.

"I'll call the Komiteh; they'll shut this craziness down. You're causing a ruckus. It's past curfew. Men and women are standing together. You're breaking and entering on city property. Shall I go on?" Hooman bows his head solemnly and motions for the man to pass to the front of the line.

"The play's the thing . . . ," Hooman mutters to his back.

"That will catch the conscience of the King," Leili finishes. "Who was he?"

"No one worth mentioning. Nothing changes."

"Even if it means that it will be the only time that we will ever perform this piece or any theater piece ever again?"

"Yes."

Hooman counts out twenty people, including the "critic" and a familiar-looking foreign woman. When the crowd won't disperse, he threatens each and every individual. "Unless you leave now I'm going to memorize your face and make sure that you don't get a seat tomorrow."

"Why does Leili look like she's seen a ghost?" Arezoo asks Hooman.

Hooman turns to examine Leili.

"Oh my God, you have no idea, the crowds . . . ," she says quickly.

"Put your head between your legs," Hooman instructs her.

"What took so long up there anyway?" Arezoo asks.

"Iranians can't form a line, always late," Hooman says. He claps his hands for them to gather around him. Leili thinks of pigeons.

"Are you guys warmed up?" he asks. Arezoo nods.

Leili sits down on her trembling hands. Her lips quiver. Her breath quickens like a rusty carburetor giving its last effort.

He crouches down with her and says, "Use this nervous energy, Leili. Don't expend it now or you're going to be exhausted by the time we start."

"I can't breathe." Leili's voice is tiny. "The guy . . . ," she whispers.

"Shhh."

Nima takes his jacket and places it over her. "You are going to be wonderful," he tells her.

"You are giving them a gift," says Hooman. He pulls her up.

He places her next to Nima in their opening postures. Arezoo hangs from the pipes, where she will screech like a bat at the audience as they walk down the stairs to their seats.

Hooman leads the audience down into the theater. The darkness acts like a blindfold on the unaccustomed. They slowly become prisoners of the dark and of Arezoo's inescapable screech.

From Arezoo's first long, piercing line, a musical note that dances off the page into a dark terminus—"Our memories, our dreams are haunted by the ghost of a dead soldier"—to Leili's last backbend, the audience holds its collective breath.

No one in the audience fidgets, coughs or breathes.

They are entranced until the last candle dies and a curtain of black descends on the space. A collective exhale precedes Hooman's voice. He speaks at first softly, then more firmly into the dark. "If you do not leave here changed, it is because you believe in your own myth."

The audience is reluctant to acknowledge the end of the performance.

Leili, Arezoo and Nima lie on the floor breathing hard. They want to scream for joy, but listen instead, first to their own breathing, then to the gasps of awed compliments, that come quickly and furiously—louder and louder, until a din takes over the dark.

"Oh my God, I'm so glad I saw it tonight, because there's no way that they won't be in prison tomorrow."

"That was amazing."

"How did they get permission?"

"Did you know this place existed?"

"It won't exist tomorrow. I can bet you it will be sealed off."

"It was too dark to tell. Was she wearing a scarf or was that her hair?"

"Did you get all of the Sufi stuff?"

"Do you think they practice in such a small space in case they have to do it in prison?"

Finally, Hooman tells the audience that the play is over, and that it is time to leave. The audience claps loudly and vehemently. They whistle and yelp and stomp the concrete as if it too can feel. Hooman had wanted it to end without clapping, without drawing that line that clapping does between reality and fiction, between those playing and those watching—between the audience and the actors. Hooman has directed his actors not to take a bow, but the audience refuses to leave until the actors at least stand and acknowledge them.

The "critic" stays until the very last syllable, even though there was enough evidence of cultural subversion in Leili and Nima's intermingled choreography in the first scene to shut down their production for good.

"I see you enjoyed our performance," Hooman says to the critic who is waiting for him outside.

"Enjoyed is not the right word. I only stayed until the end for the purpose of research. And, by the way, I've researched you. You of all people should know better. What is this that you have done to the memory of our sacred defense? You have sullied the work of your father and brother, and of their good names. Their martyrdoms paid for your education and for your mother's treatment. For the electricity that powers this theater."

"I don't believe in paying for life with blood," Hooman says.

"No, I can see that. You expect it for free. And yet, you have selfishly led your friends astray when you should have set a better example. Don't worry you will have plenty of time to be just you in solitary confinement, which is where you'll find yourself if you continue these antics. The others, well, quite frankly I'd expect it of their type, but not from you. Consider yourselves shut down. This place will be sealed and locked first thing tomorrow morning. I'm giving you a second chance out of respect for your father and your brother. I won't report you personally. But don't make any more plans that involve theater. One misstep and you're out. If I were you, son, I'd stick to engineering." He turns on his heel and leaves.

Hooman returns to the theater where the others are busy changing their clothes.

"You guys were amazing!" Hooman exclaims.

"Did anyone notice the German woman?" Arezoo beams.

"The one you were so intimate with after the play?" Nima teases. "It was hard to tell in the dark."

"Her name's Katrine. She runs a theater festival in Berlin. She's here for the International Student Theater Festival. I met her at the all-night café when she was in town for the Fajr Theater Festival. She followed us to the café from the theater one night . . . remember that night?" Arezoo looks at Leili and then at Hooman. "Mashti tipped her off when he found her hanging around the area after a play. He told her to follow us if she was interested in real theater in Tehran. I told her that we didn't have anything prepared to show her, but she gave me a card. I contacted her after I got back from rehab. I wanted to make it up to you guys. I know I can never change what happened down here, but I . . ." Arezoo's eyes well with tears. "She loved the show. She wants us to come to Berlin."

Hooman's smile fades. Nima squats down and exhales loudly. Arezoo and Leili hug.

240

"Wow," Nima says. "Wow."

"We need to leave here now. We've been shut down," Hooman says, "We can talk about this another time, another place."

"Aren't you excited?" Leili asks, "Who cares about this place? We've been invited abroad!"

"I do. I care," Hooman says.

In the morning the election results are announced—Ahmadinejad has been reelected. Three days later the country is in turmoil and people take to the streets for the first time since the Revolution to protest the election results. From the roofs they chant "Down with the dictator"; in the streets they practice civil disobedience. By mid-day the riot police are called in and theater is the last thing on anyone's mind.

بسم الله الرحمن الرحيم

In the Name of God

Tension leaks like bad air from an old exhaust pipe. It chokes and sputters until the smooth, oxygenated air pushes out the accumulated pollution from years of held breath.

Agha Jerzy promises that an actor "could bring the sacred rituals of theatre and the themes of social transformation to the audience." The audience is pivotal to the performance. He says, "Theatre became more than entertainment: it became a pathway to understanding."

Was it really understanding or just plain chaos?

A discarding of masks.

Defiance of taboo.

An opening up between the actor and spectator (sometimes called love).

Ripping off masks.

Giving nakedly.

The ultimate code breaks. The women throw off their veils. Audience members cry and hug each other. Men, women and children embrace.

Theater is the secular form of a sacrificial act. The actor becomes a sacrificial object by breaking taboos. And the audience in turn gives its energy back to the actor. It's a rejuvenating gift that blossoms into a different and better life for the actors who have alongside the audience been reconstructed, and reenlivened. No one dies. Everyone is reborn.

People think that there is no spirituality in the West and yet Agha Jerzy's theater, at the height of communism, was communing with God.

The mystics say that we can only be connected to one another and make ourselves a gift to God and to the world if we abandon our false selves—our egos. The dervish's robe drops; Salome's last veil drops. Shahrzad tells her final tale.

Prince Caspian

An orange Peykan sways gently from the end of a crane like a charm that doesn't weigh a ton or hasn't just fallen off the cliff of a mountain road to the fatal detriment of its inhabitants. The crane-truck that lifts the car to safety jams traffic for miles.

Leili looks over the metal rail at the fourteen-hundred-foot drop. It is a dismal opportunity to get out of the car and stretch their legs.

"Do you think anyone survived?" she asks pointlessly.

The Haraz Freeway, controversial and breathtakingly beautiful from the moment it was opened in the sixties, is cleared by midday and they resume their journey. They will drive farther up into the mountains and then down a twisty road into the valley that leads to the sea.

"Shall we stop and eat?" Nima asks.

"I'm famished," says Leili. Her favorite part of the Caspian Road is this little strip of roadside stalls at the top of the mountain that sell fresh fatty local yoghurt that she likes to eat with potato chips.

They disband in different directions. Arezoo heads to the fruit seller for a sheet of especially round and perfectly amber-colored *lavashak*: sweet and salty, the pressed fruit tingles the tongue with delight.

Leili and Hooman buy yogurt and chips while Nima waits for kabobs and talks on his mobile.

Nima hangs up his phone and says, "We should be in Tehran."

"To what end? You saw for yourself how quickly things got violent," Arezoo says.

"Besides, we're on an informal probation," Leili reminds him.

"I know," Nima says.

"What did your mom say?" Arezoo asks.

"That it's pandemonium down there. She periodically opens the gate to let the protestors rush in for protection."

"Let's get a move on. It may seem calm here now but the riots could catch on in the Caspian," Hooman tells them.

Back in the car, Arezoo navigates the little roads like the back of her hand.

Almost to the sea, Arezoo slows the car. "Komiteh roadblock," she announces.

"Shit," says Nima.

"At least none of us is wearing protest green," Leili says.

"Here's our story: Nima and I are married, Leili and Hooman are engaged. If we tell them that Leili's my cousin visiting from abroad and we want her to see the good Iran, they won't care that there isn't an engagement certificate. Leili, speak English if they ask you anything," Arezoo orders.

"My accent stinks," Leili says.

"You think they'll notice?" Arezoo laughs.

Arezoo pulls up and rolls the window down and hands the young, acne-faced Komiteh officer a notarized letter from Nima's dad. "Permission to use the car and the villa," she says.

"Relations?" the Komiteh officer demands.

Without skipping a beat Arezoo says, "He is my husband. The young woman is my cousin from England. She's here to marry my husband's friend. We are taking her to our villa to show her the beauty of this wonderful country." She whispers, "We don't want her exposed to all the political craziness in Tehran."

"Marriage certificate," the man extends his hand.

"We haven't had a family gathering yet."

"Temporary marriage license."

Leili's heart pounds wildly in her chest. She is about to say something in English when Arezoo reaches into her purse and pulls out an official-looking certificate of temporary marriage.

The Komiteh officer looks at the certificate and hands it back to Arezoo. He waves them on. No one asks Arezoo why or how she has a temporary marriage certificate. Only Nima says, "Thank God he didn't ask for my ID." The implication is clear enough. Nima's name is not the one on the certificate.

The familiar town mosque with honeycombed architecture constructed from old chipped tiles and decorated with a string of lightbulbs welcomes them back to the quiet little seaside town.

On the front steps of the local mosque a guard hunches over a small kerosene fire, tending to a pot of tea. A sugar cube bulges out of the side of his mouth when he smiles and waves at them driving by.

"It was nice of your family to lend us the villa again," Leili says.

"Are you kidding? When they heard what happened they insisted we leave town immediately. My father's busy bribing officials to keep us off of government records." Nima solemnly adds, "like a no-fly list."

"If it weren't for the protests I'd be on a no-fly list. My mother is thrilled to have me out of Tehran. She's scared," Leili says. Hooman gives her a sympathetic look.

"How's your dad?" Nima asks.

"Home, but not well."

After three days of avoiding the streets and possible protestors and the police, they are relieved to be in a town they can stroll in. Nima pulls the car over.

"Let's stretch our legs."

"The sky is so dark," Arezoo comments as she slides out of the car.

"It smells like rain coming," Leili says.

"Good, I need a shower." Hooman laughs and takes Leili's hand.

"We don't have umbrellas," Arezoo says.

"So?" Nima says.

"Let's get ice cream," Leili squeals.

Hooman smiles.

Cold air rises from layers of lime, banana and strawberry ice cream that twists and turns to a thin point, at which it volcanically melts down the side of the cone and into tiny bubbles of sticky pink that drip down Leili's fingers.

Arezoo throws her messy, half-eaten cone out and says, "You guys go ahead without me." She turns away from them and walks rapidly toward a yellow phone booth.

"Wimp," Nima says laughing, "Taking shelter in a phone booth, real original."

"I think she's actually making a call," Leili defends her. Nima's smile fades.

A loud clap of thunder shakes leaves off a nearby tree. Minutes later, sheets of water whip through and pink puddles of ice cream melt into the wet dark.

"We can outrun it!" Leili screams, laughing, already darting into the night.

Their pace quickens with each new bolt of lightning. They reach a rusty little bridge surrounded by water and open space just as a lightning bolt skids across the sea.

"And to think that we were afraid of putting on a little play. Nature in the end is the more powerful one," Hooman says.

"And sometimes as unjust," Leili responds.

"It's supposed to be summer," Arezoo breathlessly yells into the loud storm. She runs to catch up with them.

"Where have you been?" says Leili.

"In a hole in the ground." They laugh, thankful to be out in the open, thankful for fresh air and empty streets, thankful for an impersonal danger.

Leili pulls her russari off and runs. "Mercury, dangerous and unstoppable!" she yells.

Hooman regains his director's footing and comes alive. "Stop!" he yells breathlessly.

They slow down and look back at him.

"Come on, it's dangerous," Leili calls to him.

"The Komiteh are like rats. They only come out in dry weather. This is the perfect time to perform out in the open!"

Nima laughs. "You're kidding?"

Arezoo says, "He's right, God, he is right." She spins around in the rain and sings at the top of her lungs.

They run through the rain, lunging, spinning and rolling until they are as wet and dirty as stray dogs in a storm.

A woman they hadn't seen walking with a toddler in a thick plastic raincoat stops to clap.

They laugh, surprised. They take a bow and scatter toward the car, shouting and singing all the way.

The cook fries fresh fish from the market for their dinner and serves it with herbed rice and a twist of lemon from the citrus grove. They retire to the main room of the villa, a large area covered in rugs and poshties, a couch and an eighteen-foot vaulted ceiling. Arezoo and Nima stretch out on the floor and play backgammon late into the night while Leili and Hooman curl up with a shared book in front of the fireplace. The rhythm of the rain hitting the tin roof of the A-frame lolls them to sleep.

They wake to the smell of wet grass and fresh bread. The cook prepares an omelet and Turkish coffee.

"I read cups," Arezoo tells them.

"What's the obsession with the future when we haven't even figured out the present?" Hooman comments.

"It's a way to guide us in the present," Arezoo answers.

"Not really. By the time you figure it out, it's already gone," Hooman tells her.

"I also read palms," says Arezoo.

Leili looks doubtfully down at her palms, smiles and reaches for one of the small delicate three-sip-size porcelain cups. She places her lips on the gold rim and in one swig and two seconds downs her future. She scrunches up her face like a child tasting bitter medicine.

"Yuck, I wasn't expecting so many grounds."

Arezoo laughs. "It's necessary for a good reading." Leili can't help making a face or secretly making a wish.

"Now remember, place the saucer on top and turn the whole thing over toward your heart," Arezoo demonstrates.

Leili follows Arezoo's instructions, then hands her the cup. Arezoo peers into the cup, slowly turning it side-to-side, careful to look at the edges, the walls and the bottom of the cup. "I see an airplane, a woman waiting. You aren't married and are an only child."

Leili raises an eyebrow. "You already know all of this."

In her Islamic Republic Broadcaster voice—back from its long hibernation—Arezoo reports, "Love, a marriage." Leili blushes.

"Is he tall? College educated? An artist?" Hooman winks at Leili.

Arezoo ignores him and says, "Your plan will need another's help—someone who understands alienation, homelessness."

Hooman studies Leili with sudden interest. "Plan?"

Leili shrugs her shoulders.

"Fortune-telling is a scam. It takes away free will," Hooman says. He eyes Leili suspiciously.

"Not at all. Take palm reading, for instance. The left palm is the future and the right, the past," Arezoo says with authority.

"What if mine look the same?" Leili offers her palms to Arezoo, who takes them and caresses the faint lines. She says, "You allow destiny to make your decisions for you; instead of forging ahead, you wait and watch."

"What about collective destiny?" Leili asks. She picks up her coffee cup and glances at the remaining coffee grounds. "What about our future as a group? Our plans?"

Hooman fidgets with his lighter and drags on his half-finished cigarette.

"I have no idea. Don't look at me that way," he says.

The group falls silent.

Leili studies the drama of the sun play out against a glass vase similar to one she saw recently in the glass museum, where the light hit the vase at just the right angle to stain the wall behind it with red veins. Alone in the museum one afternoon, she walked slowly and methodically from case to case, admiring the beautiful blown glass objects while absently, she dragged her index finger across the edge of the casements and collected a fine fuzz of dust. The chunks of foggy blue and green glass looked like the tiny pieces of sea glass that wash ashore along the Caspian coastline.

"Museums are always so empty here." Leili breaks the tentative silence. No one answers. She stares down at her empty coffee cup, looks at the stain of the grounds and thinks about broken shards of glass.

"Tehran is full of beautiful objects that no one ever looks at," Arezoo says.

"Like our theater," Leili remarks.

Hooman stares into his coffee cup and says, "Leili, please."

"What choice do we have but to go to Berlin?" she asks.

"We'll find another place." He looks up at her.

"Hooman, it's over. We're not allowed to perform here." She pushes back her chair but doesn't get up.

Arezoo nods in agreement.

"We could at least continue to practice while we're here," Nima suggests.

"But first," Arezoo says, jumping up, "I've made some costumes."

Arezoo brings her knapsack and sits down in the middle of the salon floor, turns the bag upside down and from the lower depths pulls out vibrantly colored pieces of material and holds them up for scrutiny.

"A yellow ship sail? A green banner? A purple cape? A red tent?" Hooman teases as she floats each new creation out of her bag like a magician.

"No, silly, look." She takes the first yellow cloth and pulls it over her clothes, stands, lifts one leg behind her and stretches her arm in front of her into an arabesque. The yellow bodice holds tight to her chest while the voluminous skirt falls from her horizontal leg like a ship's sail. She kicks her leg up higher and it fans out like a peacock's tail.

"Wow," Hooman says. "I didn't realize costumes could have such an effect on movement."

Arezoo stands up straight, catches her breath and explains, "That's because you're stuck in all that black Grotowski nothingness. He's just like the government—he wants us to live in a dark hole. We need color, brightness." Next, she takes a green sacklike costume and pulls it over her head and bends into an extended plié, arms at her side, head back.

"Gorgeous," Nima exclaims.

"I can't take credit," she says. She sits down cross-legged and pulls the cotton material down around her. "Martha Graham. She was inspired by the Middle East—by our culture! Look at this one, for example."

Arezoo feels around in her bag and pulls out a gunnysack-like dress made from an Iranian batik tablecloth. She pulls it over Leili's head.

"Here." Arezoo goes back into her bag and pulls out a large glossy coffee-table book with a haunting black-and-white picture of the profile of a striking Western woman.

"Hooman gave it to me for my birthday last year, remember? When I'm depressed, I read and reread this paragraph. Listen . . ." She opens the book gingerly to an earmarked page and hands it to Leili: "My English accent stinks. You read it."

Leili reads: "There is a vitality, a life force, an energy, a quickening that is translated through you into action, and because there is only one of you in all of time, this expression is unique. And if you block it, it will never exist through any other medium and it will be lost." Leili looks up at Hooman and repeats, "Lost." She looks back down at the book and continues to read, "You do not even have to believe in yourself or your work. You have to keep yourself open and aware to the urges that motivate you. Keep the channel open. . . . No artist is pleased." She squints at the text and continues, "There is only a queer divine dissatisfaction, a blessed unrest that keeps us marching and makes us more alive than the others." She closes the book with finality and hands it to Arezoo.

"We have to do what we're doing to stay more alive. It will be hell without our theater," Arezoo says.

"Thank you, Arezoo," Nima whispers.

"What for?" Arezoo asks.

"For reminding us of beauty. We need color, Hooman, enough of the drab." Arezoo hugs him emphatically.

"Sure, we'll use them," Hooman says.

"I want to sing," Arezoo says. A tear rolls down her cheek. "I could sing in Berlin."

"You will. You are, with your body for now, and the voice will come, I promise," Hooman says. "Let's go practice."

Arezoo, Leili and Nima give more to their practice then ever before and by midday, they are broken. It is here, at the core, in a space of delirium that Hooman records the improvisations that he hopes will develop into something more. It is here that Leili can see that he might finally give in.

At dusk they walk out to the sea, climb atop a rock wall and follow the seam of the shrinking Caspian coastline away from the yellow lights of shore and into the gray. They navigate their way over the rocks and past sandbags as useful as scattered white cotton balls might be for soaking up the sea.

"When I was a child I used to be so afraid of those black flags," Leili says. She points accusingly at the danger flags. "They're so ominous. It's as if something's about to be lost forever." She pauses to look back. Nima and Arezoo have walked in the other direction.

"One summer my parents rented a place in Ramsar. We always took an evening walk on the coast. They never let me walk on the rocks without one of them holding my hand," Leili continues.

Hooman stops and sits along the shore. Leili sits down next to him and sweeps her palm over the ground in front of her. The gravel scratches at the faint lines in her palm. She takes a fistful of little pebbles and throws them into the sea.

"So you're the reason the sea is shrinking," Hooman whispers. He places his hand on hers to stop her.

"You think my little actions here on this rock make that much of a difference?" She prepares another fistful, then spreads her fingers and releases the pebbles to the wind. She looks out to the sea and says, "Putting on another play here would be an enormous risk."

The frown lines around Hooman's mouth tighten.

"What's the worst that could happen?" she asks. She looks away to the dark sea, exhales and looks back at him. "Tell me the truth."

"Giving up."

"I'm not strong enough," she whispers, wishing the night could take away her doubt.

"You are. You don't know your own strength," Hooman insists. "Look, Leili, I had to go to prison to be free. What's it going to take for you to be free?"

"Prison set you free?"

"It was a gift. I got to experience what I always dreaded and saw that it wasn't so bad. It freed me of the fear." He reaches for her hand, "To live is to take risks."

She takes a deep breath. "Hooman, Berlin's a risk we should take."

The sea thunders over the erratic rhythm of their breath. She does not look at his face—afraid of what she might find in his expression.

He asks, "What do the others want?"

"To go, to perform, to have this opportunity. Nima's father called while you were napping this afternoon. He has arranged everything, including your passport. Everyone wants to go."

Hooman's silence amplifies the roar of the waves. She can't look at him while he is thinking, deciding. Instead she stares out at the darkening shore and caresses the sand and feels for pebbles. The sand is cold yet her hands are hot.

"OK," he says softly.

"OK?"

"Let's go perform in Berlin."

Leili squeals then leans over and squeezes him as hard as she can. She pulls him up and they run gingerly among the rocks to where Nima and Arezoo amble along the sandy beach.

The sea swallows Leili's scream: "We're going to Berlin!"

بسم الله الرحمن الرحيم

In the Name of God

How do I keep myself out of her story when I know intimately and have desired as she does the life Leili is willing to fight for?

Berlin is beautiful. They call it poor but sexy and I can see why. We don't get out much without our handlers. We mostly spend our time rehearsing at the House of World Cultures. It's a bit isolated. It's in the Tiergarten Woods nearby the German Chancellery and off the 100 bus line (which we use to cheaply tour the city). The Germans call it the pregnant oyster. I call it the chaotic clam because it looks like a giant gasping clam desperate for air. It was a Cold War gift from the Americans to West Germany in 1957 and the venue for Kennedy's big speech. Its primary purpose is to showcase non-European art like ours.

A few years ago they hosted another Iranian theater director, Hamed Taheri, whose play Avenir, Avenir *was acted entirely by refugees. Taheri was just visiting but still managed to capture the pain of being a refugee.*

Taheri's work in Berlin was part of a show called My Construction Site that took place while the gasping clam was undergoing major construction. It's kind of an excuse to have shows during construction, but as I read the description on their website I realized how much I related to the theme of how we live and shape our immediate living environment. How does our environment change us? I think of our little oval space and wonder if that womb didn't just birth completely new people. The website asks about the sociopolitical level: "What meaning, in turn, does the site have as a center of life, when all around the world more than two hundred million people seek refuge and work in foreign countries and many more are migrants within their own countries?" We are refugees in our own country, homeless and hiding. It asks what rules of the game and rituals constitute sites?

It's the new big word: site. *But what does it really mean? Is it an excuse to avoid talk of home, belonging and love? At the end of the online description is the question, "What does* my house *mean to me?"*

A more poignant question for those of us who are homeless in the deepest sense might be, what's the difference between being nomadic and exiled? One, not sure which, is a choice. Speaking of homeless, Kamran came from Switzerland to help us out. Arezoo called him. After his rehab, the Swiss gave him political asylum as a homosexual. He's chipper; his new life agrees with him. He has a boyfriend and is free to be himself.

I traveled light. I only brought a single quote from Agha Jerzy and a single photograph of Leili's. They're like talismans that I keep close.

Art is a ripening, an evolution, an uplifting which enables us to emerge from darkness into a blaze of light. (Jerzy Grotowski, Towards a Poor Theater)

Leili's photo is of our theater. Rather it's of a single melting candle and a little flicker fighting to stay alive. Without seeing anything else in the frame, she's somehow captured in that single candle the whole strange, almost-but-not-quite oval shape of the room, the cement walls and floors that gleamed in the candlelight, the heap of rupushes and knapsacks and the four of us sitting cross-legged, eyes closed and ready to emerge from the dark in a blaze of light . . .

A snowy night . . . Berlin . . .
Do you write The End *at the end of a fragment or a diary whose story you instinctively know is over? Do diaries have endings? Do you say*

"The End" when a play is over? To write **The End** *is to draw a line like a stage curtain separating reality and fiction. No clapping. No ending.*

For us, the end is easy—simply put, we say, "That's it, folks—last scene underground."

The Gasping Clam

The anxious buzz of delay seeps through the heavy stage curtains.

"Where the hell is she?" Arezoo storms out of her dressing room with Nima close on her tail, looking for Hooman like a heat-seeking missile. She finds him in the wings where he slips Leili's note back into his pocket and lights a cigarette. The tiny scrap of unread paper burrows deep in his pocket like a stubbornly rooted splinter.

"The show must go on," Hooman says lamely.

"Hooman? What the hell? Where is she?" Arezoo demands.

"I don't know."

"You must know," Nima says.

"Shhh," Hooman says subtly, pointing his burning cigarette toward the opposite wing to where Iranian handlers officially await the curtain's rise.

"Are you sure you're protecting her?" Nima asks.

"One minute," shouts a German stagehand.

"The curtain . . . , it's late." Arezoo points to the man who holds the ropes tautly, ready to raise the curtain.

"Eine moment," Kamran says. He shows off his German at every turn.

"She's destroying this for all of us. She's nervous. She's always had stage fright. This is ridiculous. Go give her one of your famous pep talks. Why are you just standing here?" Arezoo asks.

Hooman doesn't move.

"Hooman?" Nima prods gently.

"Minute's up," a stagehand approaches them.

"One of our performers is . . ." Hooman says in English.

"Krank—sick," Kamran helps.

"Please don't tell anyone that she's . . ." Hooman falters.

"Missing?" The man suggests.

Arezoo wrinkles her brow. "She's been sick a lot since we got here, always conferring with Kamran and going out to the pharmacy. Nervous stomach."

Hooman looks at Kamran. "Really?" He reaches into his pocket for Leili's note and then changes his mind. He promised.

"You yourself just told us she was sick. What's going on, Hooman?" Nima asks.

"I didn't know she was running off to a pharmacy." He continues to glare at Kamran.

"She needed translation help."

"English would have done. We really didn't need you to swoop in from Switzerland and help us out," Hooman says.

"You were busy with rehearsals." He pauses and turns to Arezoo and Nima. "Look, just, go out there and don't hint that anything is wrong. You've spent months practicing, getting visas and passports and permission. I get to stay. I have nothing at stake. But do you really want to give it all up?" Kamran asks.

"You know something. Tell me," Hooman demands.

"Nothing," he whispers.

"Keep it calm, boys, the handlers look antsy," Arezoo says with a smile plastered to her face.

Nima bites his lower lip hard. Arezoo closes her eyes, takes a deep breath, straightens a few inches taller and walks out onto the stage.

Nima looks at Hooman, long and hard. Hooman stares back stoically, silently.

"You're the ultimate actor," Nima says. He turns and leaves before Hooman can respond.

"Curtain," announces the stagehand.

Arezoo straightens her shoulders, and moves to center stage. She hangs her head, and dangles her arms—like silk strings. The curtain rises and she moves effortlessly into the role Hooman created for Leili.

بسم الله الرحمن الرحيم

In the Name of God

Every story begins with this line . . . I forgot to write this in my journal and maybe that was bad luck. Well, here it is, at the end . . .

There once was one, there once was no one, save for God there was none.

یکی بود یکی نبود، غیر از خدا هیچکس نبود

Leili . . .

The days pass into silence and still no news. I sheltered my solitude for years and now I'm afraid of the quiet moments. Moments alone invite the twists and turns of memory, of tunnels that burrow their way right through the heavy bedrock and earth from Tehran toward the Caspian Sea. The road ribbons through my mind, filled with claustrophobic mountain tunnels, long tubes of darkness and then breathtaking forests, cliffs, peaks and you, standing on the shoreline smiling at me.

Our last night at the Caspian you said that the black flags along the coast looked ominous and I told you that they were just a friendly reminder that you're safe where you are. "Enjoy the safety of the shore," I said, without imagining that even then, you were contemplating jumping overboard. I wish I'd noticed the danger flag announcing your departure. I should have been more attuned. But then what could I have done with the information? Asked you to marry me—a homeless man without a job or a family?

I thought we were writing theory, a play, pretending, when you lightly suggested that Berlin could be an opportunity of a lifetime. The ultimate risk and the ultimate opportunity. You had spelled it out: "We could stay." You said "We."

You were looking down at the sand when I told you that I can't live any-where else. This is my home, my language, my context and my frame—and here I am back home, in country, context and frame, alone and unhinged.

How would I have supported us? I'm not a naïve Tehrani who thinks that the West is like some satellite soap opera or a bootleg video. It's never easy to be a refugee. I've given my life to this place, to this society. This is where I'm needed.

"Tehran weighs me down," you said. You told me that you can't get too close to the edge. "I am not buoyant. I'd never do it without you." You said that, Leili, and yet you did do it without me. I can't carry the note you handed to me in Berlin with me anymore; it weighs me down.

I'm taping it to this page with the Hafez fortune facedown so that no one will read it. It's the same poem I had engraved on your ring. Was that a coincidence or did you plan it? What's the point of getting senti-mental? Maybe the printer of these tiny scraps likes giving people hope because this poem is printed far more than the others.

> Hooman, you taught me to fly at a time and in a place where flying meant hitting my head on a ceiling night after night—here in Berlin the ceiling has blown open and the wind waits to carry us away. I will wait for you—when the curtain drops, walk out the front door and just keep walking past the lights and into the dark—into Tiergarten. I'll be there, waiting. Leili

But you weren't. When you walked out of the theater I thought you were playing a game. I underestimated your ability to act. I doubted your desire to run without me. I kept my promise and didn't read the note until after the play, when it was too late. That was the hole in your plan . . . you didn't trust that I could act, that I could pretend through-out the performance that you really were sick in bed and not running

*away. Did you think I'd turn you in so you'd have to return with me?
What were you thinking, Leili? Why delay me from reading that note if
you had wanted me to join you?*

*I can still hear the retreat of your footsteps, and the silence begging
me to ask you to come back.*

*I've been like a dervish whirling out of control. I'm Majnun. Nothing
matters here without you. The cabin still smells of bergamot and the wind
repeatedly whispers your name. The unripe walnuts respond to your ab-
sence by knocking against one another and dropping prematurely from
the tree to the ground.*

*I listen for you in the wind; I imagine you walking with me to Dar-
band and then in the orchard standing on the balcony, marveling at the
walnuts, their little buds just emerging from winter-thin limbs. I went
to the all-night café and stood alone on the corner with a hot chocolate in
my hand and watched the snow fall, imagining it landing on your black
veil, imagining the taste of milk and cocoa on your lips, imagining you
here all the time.*

*Memory is like the paths and lines on a palm, broken, discontinuous
and hard to read. I only remember how fun it had all been.*

*Today I received two pieces of paper . . . one about the future and the
other about the past. I'll tape them both here, the faded newspaper article
Nima found about an Iranian snow angel found fallen in the Berlin
woods the night you left and the other, a Hafez fortune about the green
sea of heaven, the hull of the new moon.*

هرگز نمیرد آنکه دلش زنده شد بعشق
ثبتست بر جریدهٔ عالم دوام ما

ای باد اگر بگلشن احباب بگذری
زنهار عرضه ده بر جانان پیام ما

He whose heart has been revived by love will never die
In the ledger of the world we are marked eternal.
     . . .

O wind, if you should pass through the garden of the Beloved
be sure to give him our message

The Hafez reminds me of one of Furugh's poems that drowned over a
year ago when it slipped out of my hands so I could catch you:

Oh green from head to foot place your hands like a burning memory
   in my loving hands
give your lips to the caresses of my loving lips like the warm percep-
   tion of being
The wind will carry us — the wind will take us away

An anthropologist saw our performance in Berlin and came to Teh-
ran just to talk to me about our experience. Maya Deren says, "When
the anthropologist arrives the spirits depart." Was she right? Have the
spirits departed? Is it too late? I'm giving her this letter, I'm giving her
all my notes. Maybe she can construct a story that will explain why
some of us stay and so many of us leave. Maybe she can make sense of it
all . . . or at least admit defeat.

Thank You

This book could not have been written without all of the generous people who took time to tell me their stories, help me with my research, read various versions of the manuscript and fund my research and writing. This small mention of names cannot include the breadth of people to whom I owe my gratitude.

In Tehran, I'd like to thank the wonderful directors, actors and playwrights Hamed Taheri, Majid Bahrami, Mehdi Pakdel, Navid Hedayatpour and Atefeh Tehrani, Naghmeh Samini and Hamid Reza Azarang; my theater-going pals Lilliane Anjo, Amir Nikpey, Nazanin Varzi and Nader Davoodi (who took me backstage at the *Blacks*); Sohrab Mahdavi and Tehran Avenue for bravely introducing a culture of critique for Iranian contemporary arts and his late partner Mahsa Shekarloo (1970–2014), a dear friend we lost along the way.

In Berlin, I thank Marina Sorbello for friendship, curatorial skill and generosity with her network of Middle Eastern artists, her colleague Antje Weitzel and the wonderful Uqbar Gallery, Stephanie Wenner and Matthias Lilienthal at Hebel Am Ufer, Gaby Tuch at The House of World Culture and Maryam Palizban, who so elegantly bridges the theater world between Tehran and Berlin.

In Irvine, Don Lafoon generously recounted his memories of the Iranian theater world before the Revolution and Robert Cohen shared his memories of Jerzy Grotowski at UCI.

I am grateful to friends and colleagues who read the entire book and gave feedback at its various stages and genres: Alice Andreini, Diane Pata-Cerabone, Rochelle Davis Stewart, KC McCrory-Wise, Narges Erami, Mary Hegland, Alexis Gargagliano, Jack Miles and my dedicated undergraduate research assistants Carly Demeo, Shirley Limathwalla for bravely reading the manuscript and Adrienne Nguyen and Amber Nuetzel for their studious fact-finding; to my friends Joanna Demers, Michelle Molina, Daniel Brunstetter, Susan Anderson, and Victoria Bernal, who took a peek at a sample, saw something unconventional and raw and still encouraged me to continue, and especially to John Lester Jackson Jr., who insisted that I put this work out in the world.

Credit must go to the generous institutions that made fieldwork and writing possible over the decade that it took to research and write this work: Oxford University's Middle East Centre at St Antony's College; University of California Irvine's Department of Anthropology in its School of Social Sciences; University of California Humanities Research Institute; The Wissenschaftskolleg Zu Berlin—EUME (Institute for Advanced Studies) in Berlin, Germany, especially Georges Khalil; The Zentrum Für Literatur und Kulturforschung (Center for Culture and Literature) in Berlin, Germany; and The IFK, Internationales Forschungszentrum Kulturwissenschaften, in Vienna, Austria.

Thanks to the anonymous anthropologists who diligently reviewed the book manuscript for Stanford University Press and to my wonderful editor, Kate Wahl; her editorial assistant, Nora Spiegel; my copy editor, Xenia Lisanevich; production editor, Mariana Raykov; and the whole team at Stanford University Press. Thank you, Kate, for taking a chance on an experiment and for bringing it above ground!

Also, I write in memory of my uncle Patrick Killough (1935–2014), who loved the Persian language and who pushed me to learn my Latin; of Parviz Paydavousi (1937–2014), my loving father-in-law; and Massoud Varzi (1931–2014), my beloved father. I appreciate my ever-supportive family, Jehan, Kim, Dominic, Massama, Charlotte, Manijeh and Jam, my best friend and husband, Kasra Paydavousi, who supports me in every possible way and more, and my son Rumi, lover and teller of tales.

Finally, I quote roughly from Albert Einstein: For all great spirits, young, old and of every nationality, who strive to overcome violent opposition by mediocre minds—may you find peace and light.

Director's Readings

Benjamin, Walter. *Illuminations*. New York: Harcourt, Brace & World, 1968.
———. *Reflections: Essays, Aphorisms, Autobiographical Writings*. Edited and with introduction by Peter Demetz. New York: Schocken Books, 1986; originally published by Harcourt Brace Jovanovich, 1978.

De Mille, Agnes. *Martha: The Life and Work of Martha Graham — A Biography*. New York: Random House, 1991.

Deren, Maya. *Divine Horsemen and the Living Gods of Haiti*. New York: McPherson, 1953.

Euripides. *Grief Lessons: Four Plays by Euripides*. Translated by Anne Carson. New York: New York Review of Books Classics, 2008.

Ferdowsi, Abulqasim. *Shahnameh: The Epic of the Kings*. Translated by Arthur and Edmund Warner. London: Trübner & co., 1905.

Frei, Christian. *War Photographer*. DVD. New York: First Run Features, 2001.

Gray Jr., Elizabeth T, trans. *The Green Sea of Heaven: Fifty Ghazals from the Diwan of Hafiz*. Ashland, OR: White Cloud Press, 1995.

Grotowski, Jerzy. *Towards a Poor Theatre*. Introduction by Peter Brook. New York: Simon and Schuster, 1968 (all quotes from pages 211–218).

Shakespeare, William. *Henry V*. Edited by Gary Taylor. Oxford: Clarendon Press, 1982.

Smith, A. C. H. *Orghast at Persepolis: An Account of the Experiment in Theatre Directed by Peter Brook and Written by Ted Hughes*. London: Methuen, 1972.

Wangh, Stephen. *An Acrobat of the Heart: A Physical Approach to Acting Inspired by the Work of Jerzy Grotowski*. New York: Vintage Books, 2000.

Wolpé, Sholeh, trans. *Sin: Selected Poems of Forugh Farrokhzad*. Foreword by Alicia Ostriker. Fayetteville: University of Arkansas Press, 2007.